The

Thought Leader Formula

*Strategically Leverage Your Expertise
to Drive Business & Career Goals*

Robin Farmanfarmaian

The

Thought Leader Formula

Strategically Leverage Your Expertise to Drive Business & Career Goals

Editors: Nikki Van Noy, John Vercher, and Joshua Owens

Cover Design: Scribe Media

Interior Design: 3SIXTY Marketing Studio - 3sixtyprinting.com

Indigo River Publishing
3 West Garden Street, Ste. 352
Pensacola, FL 32502
www.indigoriverpublishing.com

Outliner: Karla Bynum

Ordering Information:

Quantity sales: Special discounts are available on quantity purchases by corporations, associations, and others. For details, contact the publisher at the address above.

Orders by US trade bookstores and wholesalers: Please contact the publisher at the address above.

Printed in the United States of America

Library of Congress Control Number: 2019935005

ISBN: ISBN: 978-1-948080-80-4

First Edition

With Indigo River Publishing, you can always expect great books, strong voices, and meaningful messages. Most importantly, you'll always find . . . words worth reading.

"The ultimate form of career insurance is becoming known as an expert–but that doesn't happen by accident. Robin's book lays out a clear, effective strategy executives can follow to become recognized in their industries."

–Dorie Clark, author of *Stand Out* and *Reinventing You,* and adjunct professor, Duke University Fuqua School of Business

"Everyone is a genius in some way–your ideas and brain are your superpower. If you want to learn how to broadcast your superpower to the right people and achieve your goals, you need this book."

–Jim Kwik, CEO and founder of Kwik Learning

"Whether you're ready or not, technology is rapidly changing the way we all work. My friend Robin Farmanfarmaian's new book, *The Thought Leader Formula,* is a plan and path for making sure you can stay ahead of change and make massive progress. In it, Robin shows you how to reach your bigger goals, create multiple streams of income, market yourself more effectively, increase your confidence and credibility, manage your time, network, present on stage, and a lot more. If you want to succeed now and in the future, read Robin's new book."

–Joe Polish, founder of Genius Network and Genius Recovery

"Robin has turned herself into a major speaker, author, celebrity and entrepreneur in health care—all in a very short amount of time. But she didn't achieve that status by luck, and she overcame very significant obstacles on her way. She became a thought leader using a systematic program she developed herself. But if you want to have that kind of an impact, you don't have to do it yourself—Robin has written this great book as a manual for you to follow."

–Matthew Holt, founder, The Health Care Blog; cofounder, Health 2.0 Conference

"Having known Robin for over six years, I've watched her build her own speaking and thought-leadership career from scratch. If you want to learn how to effectively package and communicate your ideas, Robin's book is a great resource!"

—Shirley Bergin, chief operating officer and chief marketing officer of TEDMED

"If you have a message to share with this world, you need this book. Period."

—Kara Goldin, founder and CEO of Hint, Inc.

"There's a secret to being successful, and it's not what you think. it isn't because of your upbringing, your race, your gender, your current income level, or the schools you attended. It's available to anyone, and it's a learnable skill. You become successful by becoming a thought leader, and in *The Thought Leader Formula,* Robin gives you the exact process to do this. Whether you are an employee or an entrepreneur, new to the workforce, or a seasoned veteran, you will want to grab this book, devour it cover to cover, and implement what Robin says!"

—JJ Virgin CNS, CHFS, founder, Mindshare

"Thought leadership is a foundational aspect of every company's marketing strategy. Robin's easy-to-follow instructions will help you create a platform to launch your own successful thought leadership plan, starting today."

–Jennifer Hudye, founder, Conscious Copy & Co

"Robin's meteoric rise into a globally recognized speaker, influencer, and advisor is the result of her entrepreneurial mindset, strategic networking, and fierce determination. In her latest release, she distills years of experiential learning into a highly organized and refreshingly hype-free roadmap that gives you step-by-step guidance to increase your visibility and profit from your hard-earned expertise. This book is easily poised to be the go-to manual for thought leaders on the rise."

–Erin Matlock, author of Worth It, founder of Upbrain

"In today's world, thought leadership is a critical strategy for inspiring change and human progress. As an expert thought leader and innovator herself, Robin provides clearly defined strategies for other leaders. This book is an excellent resource for anyone who wants to spread their ideas in a transformative and purpose-driven way."

–Raya Bidshahri, founder & CEO of Awecademy

"One of the most powerful ways to build your career is by becoming a thought leader or speaker. Robin's book is a go-to guide to get you started so that you can become well-known for your ideas."

**–Soulaima Gourani, keynote speaker;
founder of Tradeconductor**

"We all want to be thought leaders—but many people are not sure how to do so. In *The Thought Leader Formula,* Robin Farmanfarmaian breaks down the thought leadership process into its key components, then tells us the key steps we need to take to get the job done. Robin masterfully intersperses her own experiences as a thought leader with simple, easy-to-follow recommendations. A must-read for anyone who is searching how to get there from here."

–Linda Popky, strategic marketing consultant and author, *Marketing Above the Noise: Achieve Strategic Advantage with Marketing That Matters*

"The ability to positively influence people is a powerful and effective tool in the world of business. Robin does a great job laying out everything you need to start building your thought leadership and begin influencing people that matter to you."

–John Hall, cofounder of Calendar.com and Influence & Co.

"Robin breaks down a complete list of ways you can leverage and profit from your expertise. She gives you a simple step-by-step process to make sure you set yourself up for success. If you take action on everything Robin outlines, you will regularly come back to this book as a reference guide to help you know what to do next."

–Shari Alexander, persuasiveness coach, speaker & writer

Robin Farmanfarmaian is the real deal. Her book will help you rise above the noise of your market and get away from the noise in your own head. She is both inspirational and practical, giving you an exact roadmap of how you can take your business and yourself to the ultimate next level."

–Alisa Cohn, executive coach to CEOs; contributor to Inc.com and Forbes.com; angel investor and startup advisor

"I am enormously grateful to Robin for her generous guidance in helping me become the thought leader I am today. Her insights, coaching, and crystal- clear process took away any doubt or fear I had in achieving my career goals."

–Monika Proffitt, entrepreneur, speaker, author of Blockchain 101

"I wish I had this book when I started on my motivational speaking career thirty years ago. I studied thousands of speakers and read all their books, but there seemed an elusive "spark"—a secret behind their apparent success. But I know now that there is no big secret to thought leadership. It's a series of steps you need to take to build a brand and business. *The Thought Leader Formula* lays out an easy-to-follow roadmap you can use to accelerate your career success. In this brilliant and concise book, Robin methodically breaks down a formula that makes anything possible, so pick up your dreams and aspirations you left by the wayside and start achieving your goals one by one! If you ask me what is the meta secret of success? Its blueprints are found in this delicious slice of wisdom distilled from years of determination, grit, and dancing with industry giants. The author's integrity and intelligence are unmatched, and her ability to simplify the essence of thought leadership is unbridled!"

–Dr. Mel Gill, psychologist, author, TV and radio personality

Table of Contents

Of course, I want to thank my amazing family—Nick Soloway, Chris Soloway, Kate Soloway, Nicholas Soloway, Kay Ransdell, and Karena Akhavein.

I also want to thank my awesome friends, who give me so much support in life: Silvia Console Battilana, Ray Kurzweil, Monika Proffitt, Soulaima Gourani, Joe Polish, Michael Wolf, Manda Goltz, Erin Matlock, Mary Michael, Noosheen Hashemi, Catherine Mohr, MD, Raya Bidshahri, and many more.

Lastly, I also want to thank Scribe Media, Indigo River Publishing, BigSpeak Speakers Bureau, and all the conferences where I've spoken over the years.

I'm dedicating this to my mom, Dr. Wendy Tinklepaugh Soloway (1942-2008), my role model and the most wonderful mom in the world.

Woohoo!

Robin Farmanfarmaian

Introduction

Thought Leader: A person whose views on a subject are taken to be authoritative and influential.

For the past couple of years, I have received messages on a weekly basis from strangers and acquaintances, all of whom want to know how to become a thought leader. Many of these individuals are especially interested in building a speaking career. They have seen others give keynotes and think, *I'd like to do that.* Of course, I can't answer these individuals with a quick reply. I have no big secret I can share in a few minutes.

Like any other major endeavor, becoming a thought leader takes time, strategy, capital, and, most importantly, hard work. If you picked up this book, you are also interested in driving your career or business forward through thought leadership. While I can't give you a short, easy answer either, I can give you my road map for success.

Use my road map for *your* success.

My Journey

A couple of years ago, I did a deep dive into imagining the future of work as president of an educational events and community company called *Innovation for Jobs*. The company was cofounded by Vint Cerf and David Nordfors. Vint works at Google and is known as one of the fathers of the internet. The company was built on the foundational concept that, because of technological disruption, we have the opportunity to move from a task-based economy to a people-based economy. I began to recognize that more and more jobs are now created for the individual, as we as a society move away from trying to fit a person into an existing job description.

The concept of a people-based economy resonated with me. Early in my career, I realized that I could work in positions that fit me. I didn't have to stuff myself into a job description box or even apply to companies with a resume and cover letter. Through connections, people offered me positions built around my personality and my strengths.

Still, I encountered bias and bullying in the workplace, which posed a threat to how far I could go in my career. The threat didn't stop me. I knew I could take my career to the next level as I always had; I could create my own destiny, this time as a thought leader—to both protect myself from bullies and to build my career at the same time.

I was confident, as I have always been, that if I had a goal I could imagine and was passionate enough about that goal, I could achieve it. I would simply need strategic planning, time, capital, and hard work—those basic ingredients to achieve great results in work and business. If you can imagine what you want as a thought leader, you can reverse engineer the outcome. You simply need to be prepared to put in the massive effort required to achieve your goal.

Having gone through the process myself, I now believe everyone has the opportunity to shape what they do around their personality and expertise. You, too, can become known for your brain—the way you think and your unique ideas. As a thought leader who focuses on an area you are passionate about, new opportunities will open to you. The more opportunities that come to you, the greater your options will be. Your negotiating power will also dramatically improve, allowing you to create positions made just for you.

Are You Ready for the Future of Work?

The future of work can be scary. Throughout history, technological advances have destroyed jobs. But they have always created the opportunity for more jobs than were eradicated.

While the past is not necessarily an indication of the future, one thing is for sure, the future of work is not guaranteed. Your parents might have worked with the same company for thirty or forty years and then received their pensions. They might have walked along the linear path that some people still consider the norm: a good college, grad school (if necessary), and then one lifelong career, perhaps even with the same company. Wherever a lifelong, linear path still exists, it is the exception, not the rule. We now expect to change our career, job, and company multiple times in our lives.

Everything we've known as "work" has been disrupted. The jobs you considered your first year out of high school or college may no longer exist. Robotics have replaced many human workers with anything that includes repetitive tasks—from factory work to fulfillment and manufacturing. Artificial intelligence will be augmenting or replacing many tasks and jobs—from legal work to diagnostics, telemarketing, customer service, driving, truck operating, data entry, and more. In healthcare, we have already seen the world's first AI algorithm diagnostic, replacing a highly paid physician to interpret a test for diabetic retinopathy.

Across the board, most jobs have morphed and now require completely different skills. Twenty years from now, our world will need completely different skills and knowledge than it does today.

How do we keep up with all of this change? Better yet, how do we stay ahead?

You can keep up and stay ahead by being a thought leader, also known as a Key Opinion Leader (KOL), Influencer, or Known Expert. Unfortunately, you can't simply name yourself a thought leader, or put it on your LinkedIn as a job. Others must name you a thought leader. Experts in your subject or those willing to hire you for your opinions must clearly see the value you offer for themselves. In this book, I'll show you how to build this value.

Who Is This Book For?

So, here we are in a new world of work—a world in which people interact with people, not brands. A world in which a startup company with less than one hundred employees can surpass the success of a large corporation. A world in which anyone has the opportunity to influence and impact others.

No matter what position you find yourself in right now, you have a great opportunity to set yourself up for success. Whether you are a corporate executive, employee, entrepreneur, or someone with particular expertise, you will have the power to choose how to progress in your career or business by becoming a thought leader.

For Executives

Much of my experience is as an entrepreneur and educator working with corporate and startup executives and others who play pivotal roles within an organization. If you are on the C-Suite or have a role at the management level, you are positioned to seamlessly benefit from being seen as an expert in your field.

When it comes to your company's marketing, people interact with people, not brands. As an executive, you can reach significantly more potential customers or clients than a corporate brand. Social media algorithms and platforms are constantly evolving, and they now promote the individual above the company. When you're seen as a leader in your field, you can reach new potential partners, collaborators, or employees online or in person.

Beth Comstock, former vice chair of GE, used her position as a thought leader to make her company look good. She wrote a book and spoke across the country, building her reputation, as well as GE's. Melinda Richter, currently the global head of JLABS, Johnson & Johnson Innovation, attracts clients and reaches new markets through her work.

For Employees: Work in Your World

If you currently fit into the category of "employee," whether you are at the start of your career or at the top of your career, this book is for you. You can work within your sector as a thought leader, propelling your career forward by being outward facing and getting credit for your work. At the same time, your status as a thought leader will strengthen your corporate brand, thereby increasing your salary.

Maybe you can identify with this scenario: You are in a large corporation and you are working quite hard, harder than a lot of your peers. You know your work directly impacts the success of the company. The problem is, your work isn't getting the credit it deserves. Others are getting the credit, whether through dishonesty or simply because they are more vocal. What's the solution to this problem?

The solution is to become visible. By being famous for your brain and ideas, everything dramatically shifts in your favor. You are now more indispensable. Many companies hire thought leaders because they know people trust them more. As a thought leader within the company, you will attract the best employees and customers.

Whether you are part of a startup or a Fortune 1,000 company, one of fifty employees or one of one hundred thousand, your company can have many thought leaders in it. Each can be known for their particular expertise, thereby bringing the company up with them. An engineer at Google could propel his or her career forward by being a thought leader just as much as someone in sales, business development, or marketing could.

If you are an employee, everything I share in this book applies to you. You will have to work within your corporate rules, but I know many thought leaders who are successfully building multiple revenue streams while remaining with their company. Their personal and professional worlds are completely integrated.

Later in the book, we'll see why it's so important to have multiple revenue streams. As mentioned, most people can't rely on the single job for thirty years with a nice retirement fund. You could be fired. The company you work for could go out of business. By building out multiple revenue streams, you have a safety net.

Now, you may choose to go out on your own or you may choose to stay with your current employer. What's important is that you will have the choice. Many thought leaders I know have been able to negotiate their time in an organization. Because they are more valuable to the company, they can take twenty to thirty percent of their time to speak at conferences, consult for startups, or write their next book. If you are just beginning, start by dedicating nights and weekends to building your thought leadership platform. The following chapters will outline a step-by-step instruction map to guide you through the different aspects of building thought leadership, so that you are more noticeable, hirable, and can command higher salaries or wages.

For Entrepreneurs: Pull the Company up with You

When entrepreneurs start a business, they are often in stealth mode or completely unknown. The business might be trying to do something new or different. Either way, it has no name. A founder's thought leadership can be a huge asset to build the brand.

If you already have a business established, you still face the difficult reality that competitors have access to similar business models, software, marketing tactics, employees, and PR. What many companies do not have is a CEO or founder who is also a thought leader.

If you follow the steps in this book, you will become known for your message through whatever you do—books, videos, keynotes, and more. Speaking at relevant conferences can give you a major edge, as potential investors and partners might come to you after seeing you on stage. You will no longer have to seek them out. At the same time, you can pull your company up with you. Saying "Hi, I'm the founder of X company" already signals to others that they should listen. If you then have something truly interesting and helpful to say, you will build trust. When people trust you, they will trust your business.

This new status will also enable you to more easily get in front of investors who might invest in your company. An investor is much more likely to take a new founder's call if they have a deep online presence and have used their knowledge to make a mark than a complete unknown with only a LinkedIn profile and splash page for their company.

You'll also attract potential employees. Again, the best people will come to you. They'll seek you out at conferences or email the company, wanting to be involved in some way. These individuals will be attracted to your company because they want to work with someone who is respected in their circles as a KOL or thought leader.

Finally, whether your company is in an early or growth stage, the right partnerships can be huge. Large companies can help your company in many ways—from developing or iterating on the product or service, distribution, marketing, and more. To get in front of the C-Suite of one of these companies, you need more than a degree from Harvard. With your status, large corporations will more likely want to partner with you.

Healthcare Practitioners

Through spending most of my time working with healthcare companies or speaking at healthcare conferences, I have seen firsthand how many healthcare practitioners have built their careers and businesses as thought leaders. Whether you are a doctor, nurse, dentist, part of a patient advocacy group, or any other patient-facing role, building yourself up in this way can enable you to share your expertise with more people. At the same time, you will attract more patients to your practice, who may be willing to pay higher rates to see you.

If you are part of this group, one key you will take from this book is the importance of simplifying your message so that it becomes more accessible and understandable to a wide audience. Then, over time, you can form a type of celebrity status in your specific niche. You don't have to be known by everyone, but you want to attract those patients who would want to use your service no matter the cost.

For Those with Specific Knowledge and Expertise

If you are a research scientist, engineer, or in the technical field, you have specific and often complex knowledge. By simplifying this information and making it useful for the average person, you can more effectively spread your ideas. If you want to progress your field or get funding for further research, being a thought leader is the ideal way to accomplish your goals. Until recently, individuals in these highly technical sectors could only reach a narrow audience. Now you have the opportunity for the world to know what you're working on.

If you are a lawyer, accountant, or consultant, you have particular expertise that others don't. As a thought leader, you are positioned to drive your marketing forward. People will trust you more, and you will gain repeat buyers. Your status will also allow you to charge premium prices for what you do.

For Investors

Because I do a lot of business development right here in Silicon Valley, I am regularly surrounded by investors. I have seen this group benefit from thought leadership.

With your status, you can build your pipeline with the best companies and the best investors for your venture fund. When you hop off-stage and entrepreneurs line up to talk to you, you can follow up with the interesting ones. You will have the leverage with your higher profile. And because companies will fight to be a part of your portfolio, you will have a stronger negotiation position. You know that the best investors provide a lot more than only money; they have a large network of potential partners. By being a KOL, you will have open doors to these potential partnering channels.

Start with *Why*

You can't call yourself a thought leader; others have to give you this title. The process of becoming known as a thought leader requires serious time and investment. In my case, it also required revealing a secret I'd kept for over twenty years. I knew that if I wanted to become a professional speaker, I had to start by telling the audience why I chose to work in medicine, biotech, and technology education. As Simon Sinek famously said, "People don't buy what you do. They buy why you do it."

If I wanted to make an impact from stage as a thought leader, I had to go public about being a chronic disease patient. I had to begin sharing about the forty-three hospitalizations and six major surgeries. Until I started speaking, I had hidden my health from everyone, but my inner circle. I was worried about it impacting my employability. I didn't want people to treat me as less capable because I have Crohn's disease. Fortunately, by this time I had already accomplished a lot in Silicon Valley. So, if I was ever going to go public with my secret, this was the perfect opportunity.

Knowing I would be seen so publicly now, I had to have strong *whys*. My three *whys* reminded me to keep pressing forward. As you read through my list below, consider what your *whys* are—those things that will drive you forward when things get tough.

My First *Why*

Whenever I make a big decision, I prefer to have three solid reasons why I have made this decision. My first *why* was to drive my business goals. As a business development professional, getting in the door is a hard step. Anyone who has worked in biz-dev or sales knows that. Cold calling doesn't work, especially for the types of projects I work on, like selling six-figure education packages, finding partners to codevelop a pharmaceutical, and raising funding for a medical device.

I needed credibility or a direct relationship. I knew that the higher my profile was, the easier it would be to make my way to the decision makers inside investment funds, pharma companies, corporate C-Suites, and more. At the same time, I was driving my career goals. I could jump offstage and talk to potential business, funding, or distribution partners, or even close a sale right there and then.

I also knew speakers get into a lot of events for free, and some conferences will pay their travel and hotel expenses. As a speaker, I could potentially gain admittance to events that most people will never have access to attend. Early-stage companies, the types I have worked for, don't typically have large budgets for employees to go to conferences for business development or sales. As a speaker, I didn't need that budget.

My Second *Why*

My second *why* was simply to create another revenue stream. You'll see why this is important to me throughout the book. I believe in having five to fifteen revenue streams at any given time—not only because of the future of work and because any job or business can be gone tomorrow, but because I am an early-stage entrepreneur.

My next paycheck is never guaranteed, so it's best to be diversified. Just as no corporation would expect to live off of one client, I don't expect to live off of one revenue stream.

My Third *Why*

My third *why* was to come at the gender bias I experienced from a position of strength. Being a petite, blonde woman in Silicon Valley is not easy. When I came head-to-head with male coworkers, some full on sabotaged me—repeatedly deleting me from a company website (I had to ask the CEO to intervene to get my name back up each time), taking credit for my work, or even calling me names in front of clients.

I was also subject to sexual abuse, sexual harassment, and gaslighting. At one point, a company attorney—who outweighs me by one hundred pounds and is fourteen inches taller than I am—put his hands all over me while squeezing me multiple times at a company event, within minutes of meeting him. This happened in front of a mostly male team. The CEO finally told the man to stop touching me, but for two years I shook with anxiety every time I saw that attorney.

I have experienced unfair treatment as a woman. As a business development professional, I set up meetings between company CEOs and my contacts—

for partnerships, sponsorships, large customers, education packages, funding, and more. In most cases, the CEO and one other person would come to a meeting I set up with my contacts. In many cases, I had known these people for years, and some of my contacts were close friends. Even so, in some meetings I was told by the men I was representing that I wasn't allowed to talk. Of course, this was ludicrous. I'm a trained saleswoman and negotiator. I have years of experience with business development. The inexperienced entrepreneurs, who had little to no prior healthcare, sales, business development, or negotiating experience, still felt they should silence me.

If you are a woman reading this book, you have likely experienced similar situations. You know what it feels like to be in a brainstorming session and speak up, only to see people respond when a man says the same thing minutes later. You know exactly what Sheryl Sandberg means in her book *Lean In*, when she states, "Success and likability are positively correlated for men and negatively for women. When a man is successful, he is liked by both men and women. When a woman is successful, people of both genders like her less."

Through all these situations, I realized quickly that I couldn't fight against the system. Men took the side of other men, even in the face of gross abuse. I also realized that what gave some of these men their power—besides their gender—was their celebrity or thought leader status. They were on stage, and the knowledge in their brains was out there for the world to see. If a man on stage told people I was an executive assistant, they would believe him even if they had never talked to me. To be clear, I've been involved with over twenty-five companies in my career, and I have only experienced problems at four or five of them. The majority of companies have great cultures and don't have these types of problems, but that doesn't make the problems any less serious.

After running and attending a ton of conferences, I saw further gender bias show up in obvious ways. Seeing male speaker after speaker on stage, I thought to myself, *I can do that*. But why weren't more women like me on stage? In 2015, a mathematician, University of British Columbia's Greg Martin devised a statistical probability analysis that concluded it was impossible that male-centric line-ups at conferences just happen.[1] This is by design. I believe that a way to counteract gender bias directly is by having more women at the top, as thought leaders.

---

[1] Jessica Guynn, "Dude, You Have an All-Male Conference. Time to Make Room for Women," USA Today, March 8, 2018, https://www.usatoday.com/story/tech/news/2018/03/08/women-tech-finance-bitcoin-protest-all-male-conference-line-ups/400798002/.

As an entrepreneur, I've had experience with everything from website design, to social media, to three- to five-year financial projections. I learned the ins and outs of sales and marketing, negotiating for six- to eight-figure deals, as well as managing professional speakers. As an event expert, I've worked every position of a conference or event except AV. In each case, I was always the one behind the scenes—working with, identifying, or building up thought leaders. Being inside of that world for years allowed me to thoroughly study it.

I decided to create a five-year project plan to become a thought leader and professional speaker. I would no longer be tied down to one company. I would no longer work more than others and still not get the credit I deserved. I would no longer be sexually abused and pushed down by men in power over me.

In every aspect of my life, I want to come at things from a place of positivity and power. I don't want to fight battles that can't be won. With the reality of gender bias, and the fact that trying to fight against it can be at best, futile and at worst, damaging to the victim, I decided to focus on putting myself in the right position by becoming widely known for my knowledge. I support anyone who stands up to gender bias or abuse, but I decided that going this route was the right way for me to counteract bias.

I am happy to say my dedication has paid off in so many ways. After my first book was released, a *Business Insider* article quoted me:

"Your book is armor, and when you're going up against men, I'm finding it's an immediate change. I'm in a tank and they're on horseback. It changes the power dynamic."

This is the power of thought leadership. It levels the playing field and can even give you the upper hand.

I do want to note here that abuse and belittling in the workplace are not limited to females. If you're a man reading this book, others might still be taking credit for your work, or you might have undergone some type of abuse as well. My goal is not to lecture on the #MeToo movement. My goal is to show other people how to win and succeed in the face of bias or abuse without confrontation or fighting.

To be clear, I've been involved with over twenty-five companies in my career, and I have only experienced problems at four or five of them. The majority of companies have great cultures and don't have these types of problems, but that doesn't make the problems any less serious.

What Are Your *Whys*?

At the end of each chapter, I will provide you with workbook action items so that you can implement what I share with you right away. Here is your first action item: Grab a pen and set a timer for five minutes. It's time to write down your *whys*.

Maybe you resonate with what I shared, or perhaps your *whys* are completely different. Whatever the case might be, I encourage you to establish your reasons for pursuing thought leadership. The right motivation is key. You need it to keep going.

So, take five minutes to write out your *whys*. There's no need to limit yourself to three or to force yourself to come up with more than one. The goal of this book is to help you design the life and career that is perfect for you. So personalize your *whys* to you.

What to Expect as You Continue

Some people like to read, skydive, hike, play sports, go to the movies. I like creating instruction manuals and system templates. Yes, I am a little crazy. Most entrepreneurs are! It made me happy to create a manual I could follow to become a thought leader, and now I am laying it all out for you, so that you can build your own thought leadership platform that works for you—whatever your *whys* and whatever your goals.

> A thought leadership platform is the foundational aspect of your unique ideas. You build *from* your platform. For example, my platform in healthcare is patient empowerment. I build from there. In writing this book, I am building my platform around empowering people to leverage their expertise to drive business and career goals. I build from there.

In each chapter, you will find step-by-step practical instructions for becoming a thought leader. At the end of each chapter, I will offer a few final thoughts and a list of workbook questions to answer. You can either grab your computer, a pad of paper, or download the free workbook with all the questions on my website, robinff.com. The workbook includes all the questions from the end of the chapters, with space for you to type or handwrite your answers.

Writing your ideas down while reading the book serves an important purpose. By writing down your answers, you can begin to form a real plan of action for yourself that you can execute on. As with any business plan, you need a system in place. No one

Chapter 1

· · · · · · · ●   ● · · · · · · ·

Defining Your Goals

As you pursue the path of thought leadership, you must begin by developing clear goals and a clear vision for how to achieve those goals. Your goals should be far-reaching so that they will inspire you to take action each day. You might have a goal of getting a $25,000 raise at your job or launching a new product with your startup. Those are excellent short-term goals, but now you need to think about the big picture. Where do you ultimately want to go as a thought leader, or in your career? What does that full painting look like?

The more of the big picture you can see, the more you know where you want to go. By using this book to reverse engineer the entire process for you, you

THE THOUGHT LEADER FORMULA

will efficiently and effectively build your platform one step at a time.

Welcome to *You, Inc.*

Before you consider your goals, it's important to understand what it is we are trying to accomplish. I look at, and even refer to my entire life, as *Robin, Inc.* I want to teach you how to build your own *You, Inc.*

Too often, I hear people talk about thought leadership as its own entity. They treat it like a separate being that takes away their resources. Because they view it as a waste of time and money, many entrepreneurs fail to be thought leaders. Others see it as a particular aspect of their lives. They keep private social media accounts for their "private" lives, and then they keep another social media account open to the public. Why bifurcate your life that way?

While you might prefer to have different accounts, I've found that having to maintain separate online lives gets exhausting. Plus, it can come across as inauthentic and not transparent enough.

There are *always* potential clients, customers, employers, partners, or investors who might have access to what you think is your private feed. You might become lax in what you share if you think "only" your close friends will see a particular funny or embarrassing post. So, keep it simple. Make all your feeds help you reach your goal, and then you don't have to worry about who can see what.

In Chapter 10, titled "Time Management," we will discuss how to bring tasks from your office and everyday life together, so that you can be much more efficient. When everything you do—how you spend your time, what you do on social media, and how you go about getting chores accomplished—falls under the same goals, you can propel forward toward your goals much more quickly.

The best way to succeed is to think of everything you do on this journey as an investment in you. The same way getting a degree is an investment in you. When you spend money to develop yourself as a thought leader, you're also spending money to develop yourself as a person. That, in turn, drives your revenue channels and overall goals, all coordinating to create the life that is perfectly designed by you, for you. In Chapter 3, we'll talk more about how to view thought leadership as a real business. For now, I want you to consider this overarching goal of creating *You, Inc.* What does that mean for you?

Start with Your Skillset and Build

To build toward your goal, you need a clear understanding of your skillset. Consider your natural skills. Are you great at engineering, sales, marketing, operations, processes? What did you study? What skills do you use in your job now that you love to use?

I am a born entrepreneur and saleswoman, and love to figure things out and pave new ways. My natural abilities include sales, storytelling, and exciting people at the idea of something new. As I mentioned in the introduction, a position was created for me, based on my skillset and personality, for every job I've ever had. Maybe you've also recognized how you can build your work around you. Now we're taking things to the next level.

Here's my encouragement: you already have what you need to begin; you simply have to take the first step.

> **You already have what you need to begin; you simply have to take the first step.**

Throughout this book, I emphasize again and again the importance of both honing the skills you have and developing new skills. To be a thought leader, you need to show up with excellence and credibility. You need to provide real value to others. I proactively and continuously hone, develop, or learn new skills that can help me succeed with *Robin, Inc.*

At the end of this chapter and in the workbook, you'll be identifying those skills you already have and the ones you want to have. Once you identify those skills, you can more easily map out the paths you can take to get to your goals. You can also identify how your current and future skills can be monetized. I choose to work with companies that needed business development, strategy, sales, marketing, or coaching, because I knew I had those skills and could monetize them.

Final Notes

Let's review what we've covered so far. Coming up with a big goal is the first step to this entire system. What is important to you, what drives you? Try sculpting a goal that encapsulates your why. Consider this question: what do I want to achieve in my lifetime?

Next, you want to identify your skillset. In what areas do people say you excel? These skills may not be connected to your current area of work or study. Maybe a friend has pointed out that you're extremely organized. Maybe you notice that you love to tell stories. To support you in this process, jot down your professional history and educational background. You might find some hidden skills there that you had forgotten about.

When you go through the exercise below, you'll want to make a list of a minimum of three to five skills you have. And then you want to consider how to monetize those skills. For example, you could monetize your skillset as a physician by: seeing patients in the clinic or by concierge medicine; consulting or being employed by corporations; keynote speaking; doing research and teaching; holding a government position or being an expert witness. If you are a naturally organized person, you could monetize that skill by working as a consultant or employee in operations. You could work in management, as a chief operating officer or director of operations. You could do event planning or project management. You would do well in any work in which multiple things are happening at once and you need to be able to keep the details straight.

In both of the examples above, being a thought leader will open more doors for you. You will be able to leverage your status to ask for more money. Furthermore, you can now pursue multiple revenue streams with your unique skillset as a thought leader, even if that is only to add on the occasional speaking gig.

Once you have identified your current skills and how to monetize them, consider the skills you want to have. The possibilities are endless. Do you want to code? Do you want to sell? Do you want to be a data scientist? Regardless of your age or experience, you can acquire new skills, but you have to want it enough and put in the work to make it happen. So, list the skills you can develop and connect to your overarching goal.

In addition, it's important to think about skills you need to have to be a thought leader in your area. What expertise do you need to integrate? How might you need to stay ahead of technological changes? Do you need to understand AI? If you were without certain skills, how would that hinder you in this journey?

Keep in mind that each chapter of this book builds on previous ones. If you go through the questions below and don't fully know the answer yet, you can revisit them again later.

Workbook Action Steps

Now it's time for you to do a little work. Grab your workbook, a pad of paper, or your computer to go through the following questions. Let's start creating *You, Inc.*

1. What is your *why*—the reason for pursuing thought leadership? *Note: reference the introduction for examples of my whys.*

2. What is your overarching goal for *You, Inc.?*

   a. What are your three- or five-year goals?

3. Identify your current skillset:

   a. What is your professional and educational background?

   b. At what do people say you excel?

   c. Are there any other high-level skills you possess?

   d. What skills do you want to have? (See Chapter 4 on how to build them.)

   e. What skills do you need to have to stay

ahead of the technology curve? (Chapter 2 will explain this in more detail.)

    f.   *Note: Next to the above skills, indicate how they can be monetized in relation to your main goals.*

4. What skills would you like to develop as you move forward?

    a. What skills do you need to have to be a thought leader in your space? Note: the rest of the book will outline specific skills you need to develop in order to become a thought leader.

Chapter 2

· · · · · · · · ·   · · · · · · · · ·

Multiple Revenue Streams

Once you have defined your goals, it's time to identify how to move forward on the financial front. What revenue streams will you pursue to accomplish your incremental goals? How do these revenue streams align with your overall *why*?

First, let's remember our conversation in the introduction about why multiple revenue streams are so crucial today—why we need to be able to keep up with the rate of change in every industry and vertical.

Technology and Revenue

Technology is sculpting the future of work. It has disrupted the job landscape; at the same time, it has also created many new opportunities in new industries. Furthermore, technological advancement will exponentially increase. What we have seen in the last decade is not indicative of what we will see in the next ten years. In the last century, we have seen unimaginable advancements in robotics, AI, space flight, the internet, medicine, and more. What unimaginable advancements might this century hold? A hundred years ago, people couldn't even dream of smartphones. What might exist a hundred years from now that we can't imagine now?

In the midst of all of this change, in a world that could look dramatically different just ten years from now, you need to keep up. Some companies have provided us examples of why keeping up is so critical. In 1996, Kodak had 140,000 employees and was a huge, multibillion-dollar company. In 1975, they developed the idea behind the digital camera, but not wanting to disrupt their main revenue stream selling chemicals, film and paper, they did not spend time developing this new digital technology. They chose the route that appeared to be safer, for at least the next five to ten years, which proved to be costly to them.

In 2010, Instagram was born, a company that seamlessly integrates with digital technology available on our phones. In 2012, Kodak declared bankruptcy. Just a few months later, Instagram was acquired—with a $1 billion valuation, and only thirteen employees.

By examining the examples of these two companies, we see a simple reality: the world has adjusted to fit new standards of technology. Companies must adapt, and if you are a thought leader, you must evolve, too. Gone are the days of our parents, when they could take a linear path—graduate from a good school, work at the same company for their entire career, and retire at sixty-five with a pension. Today, we have to be lifelong learners to keep up with the technological shifts that impact the way people earn money, survive, and thrive.

Responding to Our Current Reality

To progress in your career and life as a thought leader, it's important to have a personalized, unique platform, which paints a clear picture of who you are and the value you offer. I have seen healthcare companies hire people for C-level positions even though they have no experience in the space. Because the person has a unique platform and skillset outside of the industry, they offer the company something valuable—a fresh perspective and approach. If you gain expertise in a certain area of technology, you will especially be sought after. People will want to hear your perspective.

When you become "famous" as a thought leader and for how you think, you bolster your influence in your current vertical, but you also gain easier access to other industries and projects. You can bring your skillset with you, learn a few new things, and launch out in a different direction. For example, my main focus is within the healthcare and biotech industry, but my skillset is in developing relationships, sales, and storytelling. If I wanted to hop into another industry, my skillset would easily follow me. Of course, I would need to take time learning the fundamentals of the new industry, but the skills would transfer seamlessly.

Building your unique platform in a specific vertical will not limit your future opportunities or pigeonhole you into that career. Instead, the platform will allow you to become well known enough so that you can launch into other verticals in the future. Entrepreneurs follow a similar trajectory. They know they must first create their product for a niche, with a well-defined market and potential customer base to get early traction, revenue, and awareness. Then, once they have traction, they can expand their suite of products, grow their customer base, and launch in entirely new verticals. If you understand thought leadership as a business, you can follow the same best practices successful startups use.

Creating Multiple Revenue Streams

To pursue the path of the thought leader, you must develop multiple skills, thereby equipping yourself to have multiple revenue streams. Just as no smart corporation relies on only one client, you cannot rely on only one stream of revenue. In a time in which a whole vertical could be eliminated with the advent of new technology, you must develop multiple legs to *You, Inc.*

With multiple revenue streams, you protect yourself from having 100 percent of your revenue disappear one day. You are creating a sure-fire safety net. I have five to fifteen revenue streams at any given time, so I never have to worry if one falls through; I'll just push harder on the others. Imagine each stream of revenue has a lever. If one is lost, you can push harder on the lever of the others. The more effort you put in, the more return you get out.

I want to help you consider a few of the revenue streams you can develop as a thought leader. As you read through this list, you can sometimes use the Why-How-What formula to guide you. You can think about how each stream connects to your *why*. Then you consider how you would implement the revenue stream. Finally, you can think about what the revenue stream produces. What is the result?

Let's review specific revenue streams you can pursue as a thought leader. For each, I will provide an overview of what the revenue stream looks like in the real world. As you read through each one, consider if it is right for you.

Salaried Employee

If you are a salaried employee, have you asked yourself what would happen if your company went bankrupt, downsized, or was acquired? Where would that leave you? Suddenly, a huge amount of your revenue could be gone. That's a terrifying position to put yourself in.

Still, a consistent salary plus benefits from a job can be an excellent revenue stream, and hopefully it aligns with your *why* or can help move you toward your overall goal. As a thought leader, you can choose to stay in a salaried job long term, but now you can negotiate your pay and how you spend your time. The more well-known you become, the more negotiating power you have. I know some thought leaders that get paid a high six-figure salary and make three times that in speaking and side projects. Not only do they have both income streams, but they can negotiate how they divide their time.

Sometimes the hardest, most efficient workers are—wait for it—busy working! They aren't out in front of the decision makers in the company, sharing their knowledge. If you pursue thought leadership, you can move ahead of all your coworkers; it gets you noticed without having to advocate for yourself. It provides with protection in many ways. Now, others can't take credit for your work, and now you are the one who is recognized and heard.

If you pursue this revenue stream as a thought leader, you will have a natural platform for marketing and bringing the company up with you, as mentioned in the introduction.

The results of this revenue stream are many. You will have a consistent paycheck each month. You can negotiate a higher salary. And you can help raise the awareness of your company. These results shouldn't be underestimated.

Keynote Speaker

Keynote speaking can provide you with another highly profitable revenue stream. This is a stream that grows much wider over time as you develop your skills in speaking and build your credibility.

Sometimes when I jump off the stage after a keynote, I have a long line of people waiting to speak with me. I regularly end up staying one to two hours talking to people who are interested in learning more, want to tell me about their startup, or even offer me future opportunities.

Through keynotes, you can much more easily develop your funnel, no matter what industry or position you're in. When people give me their cards, I make sure to connect with them on LinkedIn, and their information then goes into my database. LinkedIn allows you to download all your contacts and their email addresses, which can be opened using a spreadsheet program, like Excel. It's crucial to keep track of these contacts, because you never know how your paths might intersect with theirs in the future. You might be able to support each other in your businesses in a way that is a win-win for both people.

So, why might you pursue this revenue stream? You might want to drive marketing and sales goals, fill your funnel with more leads, or simply influence more people with the message you care about most.

In Chapters 8 and 9, we will dive into the *how* of becoming a speaker and getting on stage. The results are worth it. If you're a professional, you can charge $500 to $500,000 for one speaking engagement! You are exchanging your knowledge and skill as a speaker for a specified amount of money. Once you make significant money for each speaking engagement, all the other perks, like filling your funnel, are just added benefits.

The Power of Events

Events can be in person, online, or both. When you think "event," your mind may automatically go to a conference-like setting, but with technology you can host your own event without breaking the bank.

Events are much more powerful than you might think. They can dramatically expand your market and can provide opportunity for collaboration and trades. Almost everyone loves to be asked to speak. By inviting other people to speak at your event, especially if the person is early in their speaking career, you build relationships that can pay off down the road.

An event can also create a community around your goal. If you are looking to change the status quo in a certain area, then you can leverage that community to get the word out. You can also leverage that community for multiple other revenue streams.

What is important to remember here is that an event is a business. I've seen far too many people suddenly decide to run events without any experience. They look at it like a party and don't realize they need to be ready to take a massive loss. If you run a tech company with little to no event or business training, that doesn't mean you can run an event. If you have your Ph.D., that doesn't mean you can run an event. Of course, this can be a great revenue stream, but you need to be prepared for how it actually works.

An event is a service business and needs to be treated as such. You wouldn't open up a restaurant without thinking of it as a business, so don't try to run a conference and expect to have a windfall of profits. Instead, expect to be in the red the first year. If you aren't profitable with an event within two years, hire people who know what they are doing, not figureheads who are famous for other pursuits. If you hire the right people, with deep experience and expertise in everything to do with events—especially in the area of marketing and closing sales—you will get to profit much sooner. A great events person will never exceed their projected budget and will always exceed the expected revenue. Just as in any other business, you are only as good as the team behind you.

You can, of course, start small. For example, you could run an online conference. Still, the key is marketing, marketing, marketing. If you aren't prepared to market the event heavily, don't bother. People will only show up if you invest up front. It's also important to have a few solid connections with others in your space who can help you get the word out.

Most in-person events have a small profit margin, if any. I have been on the event teams for hundreds of events—from free events with a budget under $500 to multimillion-dollar black tie events for two thousand people. For a couple of years, I was an opening night gala chair for the San Francisco Ballet, and would also help run the gala for the opera. As one of the founders for Exponential Medicine—a 400 to 600-person three-day conference—I did three-year projected financial analyses, managed sales and sponsorships, and helped run the event. I also worked with the educational event company, Singularity University, for years. We held events one after another. We would sometimes do four in a single month. Through these experiences, I've seen that most of the money from conference ticket sales goes straight into running the event itself and to overhead costs. The profit typically lies in sponsorship.

If you have no experience with events, hire an event planner who can teach you all the details. I'm not talking about hiring an emcee or a moderator who usually gets on stage at events. You need someone with operational experience who is going to answer the large amount of emails you'll receive from participants, coordinating all the vendors—from the venue, to food, speakers, and transportation. It's also helpful if they can help you with sales, running the budget, and other random tasks, like ordering signage.

To find the right person to help, do a search on LinkedIn or reach out to your network for recommendations. Do an interview with three people and see who you work well with. You'll be doing a lot together! Trust me, the time and money you invest in finding the right person to help is worth it. Think about this hire as an educational expenditure instead of just a consultant expenditure—two for the price of one!

Just like you may need to outsource the tasks related to running the event, you may need to also develop a strong sales and marketing team around you. You also need people helping in business development, who will establish sponsorships and large partnerships. These individuals will help you drive the revenue and fill the seats. Whoever you put in these positions needs thick skin. They need to be ready to hear no much more than yes.

Believe it or not, the easiest aspect of any event, especially conferences, is organizing and managing whatever happens on stage: the speakers and the content. Yes, of course content is important, but what good is having the best content on stage if no one is in the seats to listen? I see a lot of people start events and put 90 percent of their effort into content. They see this as the "fun" part and think it is really the only thing that matters. They are wrong, and their balance sheets often reflect that fact. In reality, you should put 10 percent of your focus in the content and speakers, and 90 percent on everything else. Otherwise, you will certainly lose money.

As you can see, you need to be extremely detail-oriented to run an event. You also need to know your own limitations and outsource whatever you're not good at doing yourself. If money is involved and you are running even a short, one- to two-day event, you will likely need to set aside at least two months of full or part-time planning and preparation. You will especially need focused time two weeks before the event, during which you will inevitably need to take care of many little details. In the end, events are a lot of fun, but you have to be ready for what they require: money, time, and energy.

Masterminds

Masterminds can be some of the most profitable types of events. The minimum buy-in is typically around $500, though I have seen some cost upward of $100,000 a year to be a part of. Many cost somewhere in the $10,000 to $25,000 range. Multiply that by five or fifteen people, and that's a pretty good income stream, right? The margins are much better for Masterminds than other events, purely because the price to attend is so high.

Keep in mind that masterminds are ongoing and require more of your time. They are known for being hybrids; they often consist of an in-person conference or meet-up once a year, while the rest of the interaction happens via a private Facebook group or another online platform. Ultimately, a mastermind should provide a space for likeminded individuals to communicate with each other, while simultaneously advancing each other's careers.

All this said, you should not try to run a mastermind by yourself without event experience. If you are charging $5,000 or $25,000 to be part of the mastermind, your participants are going to expect a smooth, high-end experience.

As with events, it's a good idea to bring on someone with experience running masterminds. One major bonus of bringing on someone experienced is that they will know how to predict potential problems, and to put advance safety nets in place. In the event world, there is a 100 percent chance something will go wrong, but now you can rest assured that everything won't be ruined. The participants will still have a great experience because the planner knows how to minimize the negative impact.

Biz Dev and Sales

Every business, regardless of industry, needs great people in biz dev and sales. But they can benefit even more when those in these positions are also thought leaders.

My primary source of revenue is in biz dev and sales for other companies. If you have one of these revenue streams as well, you know that you need a strong network to succeed. By being a thought leader, many people will come to you. Others who have never met you will much more likely take your call. In my world, most investors, C-level execs at large corporations, and other potential large clients will now take my call.

You will also be able to build your network through being on stage. When you are up on a stage delivering your own content to the world, people trust you. They see how you think. When I meet with people now, they know I'm an expert. They also know I have successfully supported other companies, which increases my credibility.

Consulting

Consulting can come in many forms. You can speak to a whole company, run an event for an organization, or coach individuals. You can also run a subscription for your consulting services. Some thought leaders make a full living off of this single revenue stream.

The great thing about consulting is that you can negotiate your price. Of course, you will need to be able to offer true value with your expertise. I'm usually brought in to corporations to keynote, coach executives on becoming a thought leader, advise on the future of healthcare, or to sit with the C-Suite for two hours and brainstorm strategy.

A department head might hire you for a day, week, or entire project–to work on strategy or as a coach. Pay for these projects typically ranges from $5,000 to $100,000. If you're hired by a Fortune 500 company, they can afford your full price. You can offer a "sliding scale" to other companies, especially nonprofits and startups. If you're working with a startup that has only raised $5 million to date and has a skeleton crew, they won't be able to afford your full price. I work with many early-stage startups and prefer to take whatever they are paying me in stock. Why? Because it's a good way to get stock in a lot of early-stage companies–which diversifies your portfolio. Many investment funds in the early-stage world make most of their profits off of one or two winners, and you can do the same. One big win can suddenly make you a lot of money, but you have to be in the game in the first place.

How you engage with your clients will, in large part, depend on your expertise and your personality. You might work in person or virtually. You might do hour-long coaching sessions or simply create and send reports on a consistent basis. I always personalize the consulting package I offer to every business I work with. I might offer a "subscription" package, where clients can pay a monthly subscription to be available when they need. In this model, you essentially act as an advisor to them. Another model is that the client pays a $10,000 retainer and then $200 to $2,000 or more an hour when they need you. These numbers may seem high, but in consulting, high costs are expected.

The beauty of consulting is that sometimes you only need to work with a few corporations, and you can make hundreds of thousands (if not millions) of dollars a year focusing on this one revenue stream. To get to this point, you have to first build up your platform as a thought leader. Then you have to build up your client base. But this is a great way to earn money doing something you love.

Keep in mind that technology is working to augment and replace many skills. In some verticals, a computer program, software, or AI can replace your work as a consultant. This is one of the reasons I like to focus on speaking, biz-dev, sales, and coaching; it's hard to replace most aspects of these positions. If you are going to put all your learning and growth into one or two skills, be sure they are foundational skills you can rely on now and well into the future.

The result of this revenue stream is a clear value exchange. Your company or client has access to your ideas and experience. You gain a particular amount of money or stock in return. It also grows your network easily. Just by doing your job, you are meeting new people frequently in your area of interest or expertise.

Fundraising for Entrepreneurs

If you're in the startup world, the competition to get in front of investors is fierce. It doesn't matter who you are, what you do, or even if you have a large company; there will always be a line. If you don't have "status" or a "track record," investors may not notice you above the noise, no matter how amazing your idea or product is. If you gain credibility as a thought leader, you have a greater chance of investors taking your call.

If you are just getting into fundraising and everyone on the team is unknown to your target investors, start by building an online presence. Get a website up. Publish some articles on LinkedIn that illustrate your expertise around the subject. That way, when investors check out your LinkedIn profile, they see the articles proving your expertise. Create a robust network around your content. We'll talk more about how to effectively build a network in Chapter 6.

Another strategy is to hire a business development professional or put a well-known, credible name on your advisory board. A good, effective biz-dev professional will come to the company with an existing network of relationships they spent years building. By connecting yourself with someone who can help you get your foot in the door, you gain credibility by association. You will have a higher chance of getting in front of investors and closing a deal.

When it comes to fundraising, make sure the ROI is clear to the investor. Make the partnership about them. This is important at any stage of relationship building in business. Show them how they will benefit. Finally, make sure your requests are clear. Make sure they know ways they can help beyond contributing money.

Both strangers and acquaintances email me and ask if I would like to have coffee so they can get my advice as an angel investor or entrepreneur. I usually reply, "Thank you for reaching out. How do you think can I help you?" If they can't answer that question, I don't take the time to meet or speak with them. This helps weed out the strangers who are just pinging everyone without any real idea on how individuals could contribute. This also weeds out the entrepreneurs who haven't even bothered to look at my profile and experience.

I love when people are clear about what they're looking for—an angel investor, an advisor, a consultant—and exactly how they think I can contribute. Make sure your request is clear, or people will skip over you, sometimes without replying at all. Make it short, sweet, and to the point.

Affiliate Marketing

You can punch up many of the revenue streams we have discussed through affiliate marketing. This revenue stream can also stand on its own.

If you pursue affiliate marketing, you set up ways to give others money for their referral. Perhaps you have an online program that you sell for $1,000. You could give affiliates anywhere from 5 to 50 percent of the total sale each time someone gets to you through their link, and vice versa. They can pay you a referral fee when you lead generate potential customers for them.

You can also use affiliate marketing for events. Instead of paying affiliates cash, you might incentivize them with prizes. If they invite two friends, you send them an iPad. If they invite five, they get a virtual reality headset. In this case, your affiliates are also your customers.

Affiliate marketing is all about leveraging your network to your advantage. You pursue this option to accomplish more than you could on your own.

Final Notes

Now you are going to map out your current revenue streams and think about them from every angle. In addition, you want to map out other revenue streams you would like to pursue. Do you want to be a keynote speaker? Do you want to be able to charge $10,000 an hour as a consultant? Do you want to work for a startup company? Do you want to be on the board of directors somewhere? A C-level executive? These are all very real possibilities for thought leaders.

As you brainstorm different revenue streams, consider which ones fit into your existing skillset. If you don't have the skills needed for them at present, you now know where you need to step up and learn.

Some revenues streams, like events, can be highly competitive. The healthcare industry, for example, is extremely competitive. Still, I've found a way to carve out a space for myself with unique branding and positioning. Remember to take advantage of learning opportunities in which you can observe others carrying out these revenue streams in their own lives. I was able to see the behind the scenes of events by helping run many of them early in my career. This helped me later know how to get myself on the stage.

If one of the ways you are using thought leadership is for a full-time corporate job, make sure your brand is in line with your company's brand. Align to what they think is important. What you do in your world should directly impact your day job. Make sure your company knows how your thought leadership benefits them. Your public brand has an actual value, and you need to know how to vocalize that value. By connecting the dots to your boss or your department, they will be more supportive of your endeavors when you want to go speak or attend a conference.

As you move forward, remember that you want to choose revenue streams you will be happy doing for the long term.

Workbook Action Steps

It's time to get out that workbook or piece of paper. Write down whatever comes to mind right now.

1. What are your current revenue streams?

   a. What percentage of income is each stream?

2. What other revenue streams could you potentially develop?

    a. How do these fit in with your skillset? (See Chapter 1.)

3. What revenue streams would you like to pursue over the next year?

    a. What skills do you need to learn, or what people do you need to hire to help you develop these revenue streams?

Chapter 3

· · · · · · · · •   • · · · · · · · ·

This Is a Business

Once you commit to the mindset of building a business, other aspects of the thought leader formula will start to make sense. With this mindset you understand that your business will require monetary expenditure, consultants or employees, clear goals, metrics, and a plan.

In order to move toward your goals and proactively build revenue streams that fit those goals, you cannot compartmentalize your personal and professional lives, living them completely differently. As mentioned in Chapter 1, you need to start thinking of your life as *You, Inc.* If you think of thought leadership as a side project or hobby, you will be unfocused and have less chance of success.

This is why you will hear me refer to my life as *Robin, Inc.* I view my entire life as one, with no distinction between my personal and professional lives. I understand that my life and goals are a sum total of how I spend my time, capital, and energy. What I'm not saying is that you have to give up things like family time or vacations, but by thinking of your life as a whole you can allocate resources effectively to design the life you want to live.

By identifying your main goal in Chapter 1, you can reverse engineer how to achieve that goal and align your time, capital, and effort. Thought leadership acts as a lever or catalyst to make your goal happen.

Establishing *You, Inc.*

Let's break things down into the basic components of any business, considering some of the most important elements:

- Overarching business plan

- Profit and loss statement (P&L) and budget

- Departments, such as marketing and branding

- Assistants or employees—virtual or in-person

- Metrics to measure your success

Let's discuss how these elements look in practice. What does it mean to have a profit and loss statement as a thought leader? How can you measure success? To begin, we'll consider how you can start building your business by pulling in best practices from your life.

Connecting Your Life and Your Business

A good way to think of your business is to consider what you would and wouldn't do under your "professional hat." For instance, business owners who work in an office likely wouldn't be the ones to clean it. They wouldn't go to the store to buy paper and printer ink or design the business cards. Yet, these same people, in their personal lives, are sometimes the ones scrubbing the kitchen, running shopping errands, or procrastinating on their taxes because the forms are so tedious. All three of those tasks can be easily outsourced to professionals who complete those same tasks for many clients.

In both my business world and personal world, I focus on doing what I'm good at, love, and consider worth my time. I outsource the rest. Ask yourself what you do in your personal life that you really shouldn't be doing. What is wasting your time? It's time to get creative.

> **Choose the top five things you should be doing and outsource the rest.**

Ask this same question for each task or revenue stream. For example, when it comes time for me to build a new keynote presentation deck, my time is better spent on rehearsing than making the slides beautiful. I focus on what I'm good at and hire a designer from a platform like Upwork to template a design and touch up my slides so that they look professionally done. It would be a waste of my time to spend ten hours perfecting the design of the slides, and in the end, the slides would still look amateur. When I need a new website, I hire someone for $500 to $2,000, even though I used to be a website designer years ago. I know that design is labor intensive, and there is a learning curve with every new design template or software platform (whether WordPress or Weebly), and since I'm out of practice it would take even longer to build. So, instead, I invest the money to hire someone to do it for me. A designer can do in one hour what might take me five to ten hours. I then free up my time up to focus on other tasks that I can't outsource. Or I use that time to simply get some extra sleep.

In your everyday life, what is a waste of time? Little things can add up. Grocery shopping, for example, frustrates me. I have no desire to drive in traffic, walk around a crowded store only to wait in line, then lug heavy items to my home. I choose instead to do 100 percent of my grocery shopping online—usually through Amazon or Instacart. I typically have what I need in less than two hours, with little effort.

I occasionally get pushback from people who don't want to outsource this specific task. They say things like "I want to pick out my own fruits and vegetables," or "it gets me out of the house." I counter that there is always a solution that can free up more time and energy for you. If you love choosing your own produce because you want to make sure it is perfect, you can buy it at farmer's markets, get it delivered by high-end produce companies, or shop from trusted stores that have their employees pack grocery deliveries. There are of tons of enjoyable activities you could do just to get out, including a simple walk.

Flexible Thinking + Solution-Focused Mindset = Success

Whenever you adapt to new technologies, opportunities, careers, and more, make sure you are flexible in your thinking. Flexible thinking combined with a solution-focused mindset is what will help you survive this massive job shift we're experiencing in the future of work. Pay attention to your own excuses for not doing something differently than you've always done it. Those excuses are usually barriers for change, created in your mind from fear of change or the unknown.

Like time, stress needs to be considered. Is the stress worth it? Almost three years ago, I decided to never drive again and sold my car. I eliminated the stressor of traffic, parking, car maintenance, and driving altogether. I just sit in the back of a rideshare car and work on my computer, have a phone meeting, or listen to music. That simple choice has significantly impacted *Robin, Inc.*

In Chapter 10, we will dive deeper into the importance of your time and dividing it. Remember that time is currency and has an opportunity cost. When time passes and nothing productive is done, you've wasted an opportunity to build your business. Again, go back to that question: would I do this in my "business life?" If the answer is no, why are you doing it at all?

A P&L for Your Life

When you invest in yourself and your business, it's important to understand where the money is going and how you are going to get it back. You have to consider your personal budget as a part of your overall business budget. This is especially important for a thought leader, because you are blurring the lines between being an individual and being a brand.

Like any company, *You, Inc.* should consist of departments; some will make money, and some will spend money, but they all should work together as one. *Robin, Inc.* has a branch for marketing that requires money, another branch for virtual assistants that help with busy work. I am the CEO of the corporation *Robin, Inc.*, and these are the departments.

Real Risk

When I began my career, I had two different revenue streams from working two part-time jobs at separate companies. Even when working on a company full time, I always had side volunteer or consulting work. Just like everything else in life, the hard part was going to be there first few years: twelve-hour days, six to seven days a week, plus capital investment in my career.

Yes, it was absolutely terrifying sometimes. Every day was hard work and high risk, with no guarantee of success. Even now, as a successful professional speaker, the reality of my world can be daunting. I live in downtown Palo Alto in Silicon Valley, one of the most expensive places to live in the world. I have a chronic disease. I am a petite female. I support myself without a spouse or partner to pitch in for living expenses, or to take over if times are bad.

Every day, I must compete against men, some of whom have multiple degrees, and the only money I have to invest in myself and my work is the money I make. So, if you were looking for a warning sign or a red flag, here it is:

Everything worth doing has risk.

If you're not taking risks, then you're not growing or thinking big enough to succeed. If you want to live up to your own potential, then you must be willing to approach each day a little bit terrified.

Understand that this journey requires risk. In your first year, you might not see any direct ROI from money spent. If that's the case, don't get discouraged. Even if your income doesn't explode in two to three years, stay with it.

You Will "Waste" Money

It's easy to waste significant money early on by making poor decisions. In my first year, I spent a lot of time listening to thought leaders, studying their processes, understanding their value propositions, finding out who they use for PR, websites, software, marketing, and more. Fortunately, this helped prevent me from wasting a lot of money. But even with hard core research and recommendations from professional speakers and authors, I still spent money that, in retrospect, was unnecessary.

Everything takes more money and time than you would expect. Always budget more than you think you will spend. I put aside money for those kinds of wastes. If you happen to not need to use the money during the year, then it becomes extra money you can keep. Remember, these count as business expenses. You are getting more value out of your spending than you might realize.

A Note on Hiring

In my first year as a thought leader, I used nearly forty different people at *Robin, Inc.* All of them either came from Upwork, virtual assistant companies, or companies that handle one specific function. I learned a lot along the way.

You have to do your due diligence when hiring freelancers. At times, I paid $100 and received fantastic work back in return. At other times, I paid $500 for a website designer who took multiple iterations and a ton of my time because they didn't understand my instructions.

Even knowing not all will work out, hiring freelancers can still be worth the money. To this day, I use on-demand virtual assistants from a company called Leverage, which charges a monthly subscription. At around $40 or $50 an hour, these assistants can do all kinds of things for me—from organizing databases, transcribing talks, editing videos, and making plane reservations.

The best lesson I have learned is that when you hire consultants for *You, Inc.,* know that not all consultants will work out. Just like full-time employees at a corporation may not give the company they work for full effort, consultants might not perform better simply because the money is coming from your own pocket. Make sure your budget has extra room in it for those few people you hire that don't live up to your expectations. This is just the cost of doing business. In these cases, you will likely need to pay someone else to redo the task. Corporations deal with this reality. I deal with this reality. You will too.

ROI and Timeline

Consider your first year as the year you're building the foundation. Some parts of your business will take time to grow. If you want to be a keynote speaker, you'll need to be patient. Even today, when I book a $15,000 talk, I often won't see that ROI until five months later, when the event actually takes place.

When you start out, the timeline will be even longer because you'll need to build your credibility. It might take you six months to a year, or even longer, to get your first paid speaking gig, and that's assuming you have at least one video and a developed content platform.

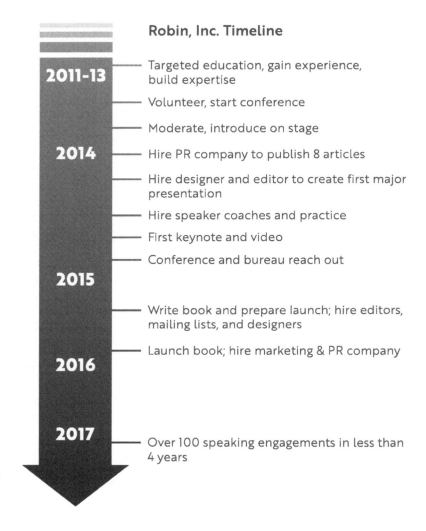

Robin, Inc. Timeline

2011-13 — Targeted education, gain experience, build expertise

— Volunteer, start conference

— Moderate, introduce on stage

2014 — Hire PR company to publish 8 articles

— Hire designer and editor to create first major presentation

— Hire speaker coaches and practice

— First keynote and video

— Conference and bureau reach out

2015

— Write book and prepare launch; hire editors, mailing lists, and designers

— Launch book; hire marketing & PR company

2016

2017 — Over 100 speaking engagements in less than 4 years

Parts of your business will take time to develop, but that doesn't mean you have to wait forever to get going. I have seen friends launch themselves as thought leaders rapidly. Monika Proffitt had been at the beginning of her thought leader journey in the first year or two of our relationship. She had been successful in the art world, but she wanted to break out into the blockchain industry. She made a major step toward this transition in a period of ten days. As she already fully understood the basics of blockchain, she wrote an eighty-page book called *Blockchain 101* quickly and easily, with little to no research.

Go ahead, write a PDF.

As her mentor, we both agreed writing a book would make a big difference in her career change, but Monika wanted to do it cheaply and quickly. So, I told her to "Publish a PDF." To publish a PDF, you simply need to write a twenty-page Word doc, and then turn it into a PDF. Alternatively, write ten to fifteen articles, stitch them together in one document, call each article a chapter, add a little commentary that ties them all together in an intro and conclusion, and you've got a short book.

If you decide to go this route, let me share another piece of the story that might help. When brainstorming the book content, title, audience, business model, and potential revenue streams with Monika, we concluded that being an expert on blockchain at blockchain conferences wasn't going to make her stand out. However, if she could be the only blockchain expert at non-blockchain events, she would have a starring role. So, when writing her first book, she wrote the basics—essentially a dummies guide to blockchain. Not only was the content incredibly easy for her to write, but it was valuable for a lot of people, corporations, and startups that wanted to understand the basics. Now Monika is one of the go-to people for events that need an "intro to blockchain" speaker.

What are the basics in your industry that you could teach to people outside your industry? That might be a place for you to start.

Nine Products in One

When creating a new platform, take into account that people pay for packaging and delivery, not content. If you write one book, you can then create five or more products based on that, each one more expensive that the last. These are called "upsells."

When creating the TLF platform (Thought Leader Formula, of which this book is a part), I knew I could easily turn this into a five-in-one or even nine-in-one deal, because it is a step-by-step process that translates well across many content mediums: written, in person, spoken, audio, video, and more.

Here are the five products, aka upsells, with the TLF platform, and four more optional upsells that I could launch at any point:

1. A workbook for the price of an email address

2. A book: typically priced at under $20 or $30, though some can be as low as $0.99

3. An online learning program: this is a higher-priced ticket item that expands on this content and engages members in a personalized way. A lot of paid online learning programs by thought leaders are priced between $59 and $3,000 in total, sometimes using a subscription model, sometimes a one-time purchase or payment plan model.

4. An hourly consulting package for corporations and entrepreneurs. This is even higher priced and more personalized.

5. A full keynote and/or workshop on the topic, typically for five-figure speaking fees

6. A community around the interest area: this can be one-time purchase or subscription

model. While this book doesn't cover building communities, there are many resources that can instruct you on launching these. Prices vary dramatically.

7. An online conference, completely variable on pricing

8. An in-person conference, completely variable on pricing

9. A mastermind conference: a hybrid between an in-person or online conference and a community. Some can cost $25,000 or $100,000 a year per participant, with a lot around the $5,000 price point.

The "free" part of my platform—the workbook—acts as a feeder to the TLF Platform sales funnel that leads to the expensive products or upsells. With the workbook, I provide value up-front in exchange for an email address, which most people see as a negligible or zero cost. In reality, email is a key avenue for a relationship. Once I have your email address, I can communicate with you about other products or upsells. Once someone downloads the free workbook and it provides value, they are also more likely to trust me and want to know more about what I offer. This is called leading with value.

The beauty of ROI as a thought leader is that it multiplies over time. You put in the most work up front in everything new you do, and then you have all kinds of ways to sell your content and expertise, simply repackaging the same information and expanding upon it.

That begs the question: if it's all the same information, why would someone pay thousands to hire me as a consultant if they could just get a free workbook?

> # People don't pay for content; they pay for packaging.

The real value difference is in the packaging and personalization. When we have a hand to hold, we can learn more and grow more quickly. In an online course, for example, you can expand and customize the material much more than you would in something like a workbook.

Whatever industry you are in, you can use this same process. Consider what your upsells will look like. What can you offer in exchange for an email address that will provide value to your current potential revenue base? How will you expand the content and personalize your approach with each product or upsell?

Project Planning and Metrics

Every corporation has a very detailed month-long (if not year-long) plan. You need to think about your plan, too. Look out a year ahead. At the very least, form a detailed overview of what you expect to do in the next month and a skeleton plan for the next year.

> **In business, if it's not metricized, it doesn't exist.**

As you plan, remember that you need hardcore, annual goals. For example, by year two, you might want to have two salaried clients and have ten speaking events scheduled for the year. You might be aiming for a promotion at work, a successful fundraising round, a new job, an email list of 10,000, or the opportunity to travel to at least five countries. The options and opportunities are endless.

Choose two to five goals, write them down, and put them in the Google doc project plan template a year out. Find my templated spreadsheet recording systems at https://www.robinff.com/spreadsheet.html or linked on my website, Robinff.com.

My favorite way to plan things out is to put things into a spreadsheet. It is an easy, cheap way to do project planning. The reason I use Google Sheets is because they are in the cloud, they have real-time shared editing and are accessible from all my devices. The project plan template on the Google Doc TLF System Templates can get you started. You can also use any other planning software you are used to using.

As mentioned in Chapter 1, you should have audacious goals. You should also have a plan of attack, or else your goals aren't actually audacious; they are just wishes or dreams. If you work hard and map out your goals, you will be able to reverse engineer your success. Not only will you achieve your measurable goals, but you will likely surpass them.

Remember that this is a plan for a business. The goals will require risk and cost. In my first three years, I spent $70,000 to build up my career. I thought of this as a way to educate myself and set myself up for success. Had I paid instead for an MBA, I might have spent three times that amount and taken out loans. At the time, it was terrifying to spend the money, but now I am incredibly happy I took the risk.

Workbook Action Steps

With your project plan template, your next step is to generate your first-year budget.

Picasso once said, "Action is the foundational key to all success." Trying to do a budget seems terrifying. You have to simply start, or you will want to skip it this step. I encourage you to set a time limit for twenty minutes and fill out the spreadsheet as much as you can.

You don't need to map out everything right now. As you move through each chapter, you'll think of more to add to your plan. For now, simply jot down the obvious needs, such as a website and virtual assistant expenses (what you will need to outsource). Some of the below expenses will be covered later in this book.

1. What is your first-year budget? Here are some baseline to premium prices to help you estimate a budget for different items:

    a. Book PR ($15,00 for three months), book marketing ($12,000 for three months), website developers ($500 to $5,000; most around $2,000), keynote script writers ($1,000 to $10,000), graphic designers

($50 to $200/hr.), virtual assistants (monthly subscription plus $40/hr.), software (like editing software; varies widely), hardware (like phone and computer; varies widely), travel ($500 to $2,000 per trip), hotel ($300 to $400/night), speaker coaches ($200 to $3,000/hr.), conference fees ($100 to $2,000)

Chapter 4

· · · · · · · ● ● · · · · · · · · ·

Confidence and Credibility

As we have been talking about goals, revenue streams, and building *You, Inc.* as a business, you may be wondering where to start. How do you build your credibility and your platform?

When it comes to thought leadership, confidence is of utmost importance. You need confidence to have a strong voice. Confidence will counteract imposter syndrome. If you are convinced that you know your stuff, then that competence is going to come through. Over time, you want to gain the ability to step on stage and command the audience's attention.

This chapter will outline three specific ways to grow your confidence: education, developing your skills as a writer, and identifying other thought leaders in your space as role models or mentors.

Hacking Education

If you don't feel like you are fully educated in the area on which you're focusing as a thought leader, a great way to gain expertise quickly and at a low cost is to "hack" your education. We're in an era where technology is disrupting and democratizing education, in which access to top information is no longer reserved for the rich or the few top brains.

While a doctor or a lawyer needs to pursue a traditional path in education today, a thought leader doesn't necessarily need the impressive letters from top schools after their names to succeed. In fact, except for a few professions, many educational paths leading to careers can now be hacked. While some corporations are slow to adopt the "no traditional MBA needed to advance mentality," in Silicon Valley, many companies don't think an MBA is an advantage, because it can teach in-the-box thinking. Many big tech giants and other innovative corporations follow that line of thinking, with some not even requiring a four-year undergrad degree for some positions.

In 2017, IBM's vice president of talent, Joanna Daley, told CNBC that about 15 percent of her company's US hires don't have a four-year degree.[2] Google, Apple, Starbucks, Nordstrom, Costco, Hilton, Whole Foods, and even Bank of America are no longer requiring college degrees to work there.

My Journey

Because my undergrad college days were spent in and out of the hospital, not knowing if I would survive long enough to even earn an undergrad degree, getting letters after my name wasn't even on my radar. Fortunately, because of a strong education background from New England boarding schools for high school, I was independent and had incredible study and learning habits by the time I got to college. I knew how to study and how to conquer rigorous course loads. Being ill, I knew I would have to get creative, and I did. I was able to complete my undergrad degree in management from my hospital bed, even without the internet. I couldn't email my teachers, so I had to come up with creative ways to communicate with them about my assignments and

[2] Courtney Connley, "Google, Apple and 12 Other Companies That No Longer Require Employees to Have a College Degree," CNBC, October 8, 2018, https://www.cnbc.com/2018/08/16/15-companies-that-no-longer-require-employees-to-have-a-college-degree.html?

to, many times, teach myself. Usually that meant reading the textbook and checking out library books to supplement.

After earning my undergrad degree, I hacked the rest of my education. Did you know you can take classes at most of the top universities, without applying or paying those astronomical fees matriculated students need to pay in order to be granted a degree? I've attended classes at Harvard, Stanford, Wellesley, Dartmouth, Golden Gate, Boston University, and Berkeley—at night, auditing during the day, or in Executive Education. Night classes are hundreds of dollars a class, meant for people with full-time jobs, not interested in earning a degree.

I took all the graduate-level classes required for a CFP degree (Certified Financial Planner), but didn't bother to get the certification, knowing I was never going to work in the finance industry. Still, those graduate finance classes were foundational to my current and future success. Since I didn't care about the degree itself, I was able to take the classes at night at a small local university that caters to professionals, versus full-time students. I paid a few thousand dollars total to take all those finance classes. I also had no pressure to get a perfect A grade. I was learning for my benefit, not because of some predetermined, rigid path to a degree.

Living so close to Stanford, that became my go-to spot for night classes. It was a $350 Stanford course that taught me to write at the sixth grade level. Those skills now allow me to simplify and explain difficult or technical subjects to nonexperts. In fact, what I learned in that class became a core part of my skillset, and I still use what I learned in both writing and speaking. For another subject, I got together with three other classmates and hired a Stanford professor as a personal teacher to go deeper into the subject with us for a year. We each paid a couple thousand dollars for this personalized experience.

Hacking your education is easy if you put your mind to it and you care more about the knowledge than those letters after your name, or the embossed piece of paper. With so many online classes available, it's possible to hack your education solely with those. That said, in-person classes or educational conferences have the added benefit of networking. Always aim to get the most ROI out of each educational opportunity.

With the internet at your fingertips, you have no excuse to not learn. In fact, you can search for thought leaders in your space and learn directly from them. Later in this chapter, we will dive into how to identify these thought leaders. With the internet, you can also get extremely specific in your research. If you want to learn everything there is to learn about AI for gaming, you could set up Google alerts for AI in gaming, subscribe to newsletters from other thought leaders and institutions, and dedicate two hours a day to reading news in that vertical. I spend two hours a day reading the latest news and advancements in my space, to stay up to date on the cutting edge.

Your challenge now is to broaden your definition of education. It's not all about the letters after your name. It's not all about specific degrees, or the best schools, or the highest educational credentials. With the immediate access you have to top speakers in your field on platforms like YouTube, you can continue learning and developing without spending a ton of money. If you can dream of something you'd like to learn, you can find a way to learn it today without spending thousands of dollars, or any money at all.

A Lifelong Journey

Education is ongoing. Learning is a lifelong pursuit. Just because you put in some work into your education in your twenties doesn't mean you will be able to hop on a stage to speak to your audience, whether it be today or in ten years.

Once you begin your thought leader journey, your education doesn't end. You must continuously educate yourself, stay current, and find new, interesting angles. Make it a point to read every day, and research the companies or products you read about. If you look at studying and learning as vital processes in your business, you will make time for them. If you do a little every day, learning can become a lifelong habit that you enjoy daily. My time for reading is one of my favorite times of the day. I love the habit of waking up, drinking tea, and reading medical and biotech news for an hour before my workout.

The Importance of Writing

One way to put your learning into practice and build your confidence and credibility is by developing as a writer and developing your initial "portfolio" of content.

Writing is a skill, and mastering any skill takes practice. Even if you get a standard advanced degree, you still might not know how to write the way a thought leader should. The more you write, the better you will get, as with anything. When I first started, it was torture. I hated writing articles, because I never practiced.

In the beginning of my career, most of my writing was around project plans, client reports, simplifying technical or scientific writing, and creating instructions. Writing an article was a whole other story! I wasn't used to it, and I didn't have a content catalog to pull from. Everything had to be an original idea. As with any skill, the first ten to twenty hours are the hardest, with a steep learning curve. Once you get past those initial hours, the learning curve flattens out significantly, as you gain a solid foundation to build this new skill.

If you are new to writing, then here is an easy way to get started: just *do* it.

Start writing with your base language. If you aren't getting your content out there in any way, no one's going to know you exist. Yes, video is becoming more and more important, but even video begins from a written concept. Furthermore, thought leaders in the business world aren't necessarily YouTube or video celebrities. What they all do share in common is written content. It's a requirement in business, not an option.

I didn't only learn through writing short articles. I also immersed myself in the process of becoming a better writer. I took a class at Stanford on magazine writing. The reason I chose that course was because I knew it would teach me how to simplify my ideas—to write at a sixth grade level.

Why is this important? Well, in the US, most kids have a great foundation in the English language once they are about twelve years old, but they haven't started specializing in particular skillsets, which require their own vocabulary. After this age, they begin to diverge significantly in areas of focus. This divergence between each individual's knowledge base increases rapidly through high school, college, grad school, and the workforce. An ivy-league-trained medical doctor with an extremely high IQ might be lost at a space conference, not because she isn't smart, but purely because she hasn't been exposed to the vocabulary and basic foundational concepts in that field. Of course, that works both ways; the rocket scientist might be lost at a medical conference.

As a thought leader, it's important to be able to communicate with a wide audience. You can learn how to do this first through writing—by being forced to make complex ideas simple. Always ask yourself: would a twelve-year-old understand your ideas? Boil your ideas down to the basic components so that you get your point across to your audience in a way they can understand.

Hacking Writing

Don't expect to learn how to write overnight, and don't be afraid to hire a company like Influence and Co. John Hall, cofounder of Calender.com and Influence and Co., was one of my earliest supporters. I met him by constantly asking people at conferences who they knew and used to help them with writing.

I asked John to share a little about what Influence and Co. does, to help you see if a service like this might benefit you. He said:

> "We know that people want to create and distribute content to build trust with the audiences that matter to them. Influence & Co. is an integrated content marketing company that helps people and companies accomplish this. We can help with everything from strategy to creation to distribution in media outlets. In the end, everybody wins: leaders, our writers, and the readers."

I hired Influence and Co. at the beginning of my journey. Over the phone, we would talk about content topics I wanted to explore. I would give them resources I had, and they would write up an 800-word article based on my research, ideas, and point of view. That was the easiest way to begin to build a content catalog, while I was still learning to write professionally and quickly.

You can also use on-demand virtual assistants. Scripted is another great company that does a wonderful job of capturing your voice; it's another platform that connects you with virtual copywriters and freelance writers. They look at your previously written work and help you write more content for a monthly subscription fee, plus a per article price. If you use a service like this, be specific with your request. Don't just say, "Write me an article on the future of work." Instead, provide the writer with some bullet points or links as references.

You could even hack your first book by ordering ten to fifteen articles on your subject matter, either with the same writer or a variety of writers. Hire a designer on a platform site like Upwork to do a cover, use a virtual assistant to format into an e-book and/or paperback according to the directions on Amazon, then upload and bam—you just published your first book!

Using these kinds of services, I was able to create my first "content catalog." This consists of four to five articles that encapsulate your main ideas.

Once you have this catalog, you can use it as the foundation for other articles. You can copy/paste paragraphs from these articles to hack together more articles. Copying and pasting, or "scaffolding," is your best friend. You can take a paragraph from one article, a paragraph from another article, join them together with a new paragraph, and you have a new article. Using this process is not only helpful for you, but also for your readers. It helps your readers follow along with your main themes. Each article will inevitably support the underlying thesis you have. Later down the road, an opportunity may arise to share an article through a big magazine or website. In that case, you can pull content from this same catalog.

Once I had my catalog, I was able to write articles from scratch, without stealing from my previous works. Now, I can write an 800-word article in under thirty minutes without doing any research or reading any of my old work. I went from being a terrified amateur to being an expert writer, and relatively painlessly.

Eventually, you will become skilled at tying any of your content together, even as you expand upon it. Your ability to tie content together will support you in other areas, like consulting and speaking. At the end of the day, you will have greater credibility and greater confidence in what you're presenting to the world.

A Note on Your Writing Voice

There are two types of "voices" in the world of thought leadership. One is based on how your voice actually sounds. We'll talk about this more in Chapter 8. Here, we'll specifically explore the second kind of voice: your writing voice.

Your writing voice is a combination of your sentence phrasing style, the vocabulary you use, punctuation, and overall way you structure information. Your emotions should shine through your writing.

While we want to focus on writing voice here, your voice needs to shine through in every element of your branding. Here are a few questions to help you accomplish that goal each time you speak, write, or present your brand in some way:

- Do your emotions come through?

- Is your voice conversational—not too academic or technical?

- Have you connected with the reader on a personal level?

For those of you with PhDs and MDs that work in science or any other degree that requires academic writing, you will need to tap into something more personal. You've been taught, and have deep practice, with technical writing. Your writing as a thought leader should be considerably different.

Again, you can outsource some of this. There are companies like Jennifer Hudye's company, Conscious Copy & Co., that specialize in putting personality into writing. Conscious Copy even has workshops that teach you how to get your personality and authenticity to shine through in all your writing. As covered in the previous chapter on building a content catalog, hiring companies like Conscious Copy & Co can help you build that solid foundation for content as well.

One way to think of getting your writing voice right is to simply speak your thoughts out loud. Your spoken voice has the emotion built in. That's your voice. It's what makes you unique and sets you apart. It's the way you phrase things and give your words emotion.

My trick? For some of my book content, I speak as if on stage or in a conversation, and then get the content transcribed. My voice and my personality are then ingrained into every sentence. I've had people tell me they hear my physical voice in their head when they read my books. That's the kind of feedback you want to aim for. You want readers to actually hear or see you saying the words.

Advisors and Mentors

Along with education and writing, you can build confidence and credibility by having mentors or role models. On my website, you can download a worksheet I have provided for free. You can follow along with that worksheet as you read this section. You can also find this worksheet here: https://www.robinff.com/spreadsheet.html.

To begin, identify other thought leaders in your vertical. Put them into the provided spreadsheet. Next, follow those thought leaders on all the platforms they have. This will allow you to interact with them. If you're following someone you have never met, you could retweet one of their tweets every week or share one of their Facebook posts. By doing this, your name will pop up consistently, and they will often begin to notice.

Liking, sharing, and commenting on social media is "social media currency." These simple actions can translate later to real-world monetization, as people with more followers than you and a larger platform than you interact back, allowing their audience to see you. This said, you can't expect a few likes on Instagram to get someone's attention, especially if they have hundreds of thousands of followers. What will stand out much more is a comment or direct message. In these small spaces, always make what you say about them, not about you.

If you have developed some level of engagement with someone through social media, you could send a direct message, ending your note with an action request. You could see if they would be willing to jump on the phone for half an hour or grab coffee at their lunch break. It can be intimidating to put yourself out there at first, but if you both talk about similar content, you likely have a natural starting point for a conversation.

Another easy way to find role models is to identify the conferences you wish to attend or keynote. Go to the conference websites and look at who is speaking. Those are the thought leaders you need to be following and understanding. When I worked at HealthTap in 2010 as a social media director, I made it a point to get to know each of the thought leaders in the health IT space, which is now called digital health. I used things like Twitter and keywords to look people up and see what was trending. I recorded those people with a lot of interactions into my spreadsheet. These were the thought leaders.

Part of my job was to put up and maintain a website and blog for the company. I would contact the thought leaders I previously identified to ask if I could republish an article of theirs on the HealthTap blog, with a link to them. Eight years later, I am still friends with some of the thought leaders I promoted on the blog. Simply because I reposted their content, I was able to establish relationships with excellent role models in my life.

As you are mentored by other thought leaders, they will pull you up with them. They will not only introduce you to others in the space, but your affiliation with them increases your credibility.

Credibility Through Association

You can gain association through a position with a company or through advising, investing, or sponsoring a company. This association can provide you with significant credibility. It is, in fact, significantly more important than your education, because it signifies you actually do something, not just study it.

One of the reasons I became a biotech and healthcare angel investor was for association. As mentioned in the introduction, I always need three major reasons to do anything substantial, especially when it concerns money. Along with association, I made this choice to reach my life goal of impacting one hundred million patients and because I knew it would help me network with more people in the space. I choose to put some of my savings into high-risk pharma to walk the talk, but association gained me some unexpected results as well.

After my first investment, I posted about it on LinkedIn. Two amazing venture firms approached me to co-invest with them when they lead funding rounds. I suddenly had access to highly vetted, funded companies. As a well-known speaker, I'm not subject to the standard investment minimums either. Companies know I bring more to the table. Finally, association allowed me to get five extra hours on stage as a startup investor judge or moderator for startup pitches. That's more time on stage than some speakers get in a lifetime—all because of association!

The Complete Circle

The more confidence and credibility you gain through education, writing, mentor relationships, and association, the more you will be in a position to give back the knowledge you have gained to others. I call this "sending the elevator back down," and I love to do this especially for other women, but I also help men as well. The way we'll get more women in positions of power is by working as a team to empower each other. Working individually, we will probably fail at getting a lot of women in the C-Suite, boardroom, or government. But together, we will definitely win.

Many of us had to crawl up the side of the building using our nails to get to where we are. There are a lot of us who want to make it easier for others to reach their goals and achieve the success we have achieved.

Send the elevator back down.

If you live your life as a giver, empowering others, sometimes help comes from the places you never thought it would. This happened to me with Monika Proffitt. We met at a conference, and I mentored her in a career transition and building thought leadership. I had no idea she would ever help me with anything. She was coming from the art world, which I knew nothing about, but I liked her as a person, and wanted to help her succeed. It was more than a year later when I discovered she was an expert on online courses and marketing, and she could help me get started with this platform. Who knew? You never know when you will meet someone or make a connection with someone who will further your interests and expertise down the road.

As you "pay it forward," you will see the return. In Adam Grant's book, *Give and Take,* he talks about the spectrum of people and their personalities—givers, matchers, takers, and everyone in between. When I saw Adam at the Nantucket Project, he spoke on how givers in the world of business are often the ones who fail the most. When I heard that, my heart faltered. I had this huge conflict suddenly in how I enjoyed living my life, helping people, while also wanting to be successful. Fortunately, this panic only lasted a few minutes, as Adam went on to explain that givers are also the most successful people.

The key, he explained, is to know how and when to give. Some people don't know when to stop giving, spending so much time on others that they don't ever help themselves. When a giver understands how to give what they actually have to give, while also making sure they're helping themselves, they can see massive success in their lives.

Final Notes

Take a few moments to brainstorm keywords in your subject area. For example, during the beginning of my career, one of the keyword's I focused on was "virtual care." What are ten keywords you would use on social media posts, if you were discussing your platform?

Using those keywords, search for and find twenty-five thought leaders in your space. Some of these could potentially be advisors, role models, and mentors. Some you simply learn from by following them. Some could be CEOs for Fortune 200 companies, and you never know if they might notice you and your platform. Follow them on every platform you have.

One other practical way to gain credibility is to get on a list, such as the *Forbes* 30 Under 30 or *Fortune's* 40 Under 40 list. Identify lists for your industry and decipher how you can get on one of them. You might need to hire a company like Influence and Co, which will work to get you on them with the content you create. They can act as an agent for you in that respect. Also see if you can be introduced to those who control those lists. The lists are essentially opinions of others. It isn't a "fair" contest by any means. There is always a third party that can advocate for you. It is a contest between who knows who.

John Hall explained this when he shared the following with me:

> "We can help place our writers on credibility lists because we work with people who already have a lot of potential, but simply don't know how to get on those lists. We live in a world of trust barriers and relationships. Contributors, journalists, and editors have learned to trust people like me and others at Influence & Co., so we find fits for people who deserve to be on these lists."

Workbook Action Steps

If you haven't downloaded the TLF Template on my website yet, either download it now, or start your own spreadsheet.

Here are some more items to include in the spreadsheet:

1. Brainstorm five to ten keywords/hashtags around your subject area.

2. List people who are thought leaders in your space, who could be possible role models, advisors, or mentors.

a. Search conferences in your field using the identified keywords/hashtags and list the speakers in your subject area in a spreadsheet. Make sure to record both the conferences with their URLs, but also list separately those speakers that are relevant for your platform.

b. General Google search, general YouTube search

c. Amazon search for relevant books and authors

d. Social media search

e. Goal: Record at least twenty-five names of thought leaders, speakers, or authors in your spreadsheet.

f. Start following them on social media and subscribe to their newsletters.

g. Identify three to five relevant "lists," like *Forbes* 40 under 40, or any of the Top 100 lists. Record the lists themselves, as well as the previous honorees that are relevant to what you are doing. The info gathering should include publication, list attributes (under forty years old, or marketing professionals, or top lawyers), contact emails, and key players in the decision making for who gets on the lists.

3. Optional action item, especially for those who get overwhelmed with email: create a new free email address that you can use just to subscribe to newsletters and alerts, so that they are all in one place for you to study and read—already organized in one place. This way, you don't have to worry about spam or missing an important email.

Chapter 5

· · · · · · · · ● ● ● ● ●   ● ● ● ● ● · · · · · · · ·

Branding

Whatʼs in a name? Roses notwithstanding of course. As a thought leader, your brand is directly tied to your name. Ultimately, your brand is the impression people have of you when they hear your name. Itʼs critical, then, that your brand stands out. In this chapter, weʼll discuss the elements that create a great brand.

A Strong Brand Is Recognizable

If someone were to Google your name, what would come up? If there is a plethora of people out there with a similar name or message as you, how are you going to differentiate yourself? When someone searches for you, you want to be 100 percent of the Google results for at least the first two pages. You can only accomplish that by having a differentiated brand people can relate to and remember.

First, you can try to "enhance" your name. Do so by adding your educational credentials, your middle initial, a prefix, or doing something else creative like adding a "the 3rd" after your name. You could add a permanent tagline, such as "John Smith: The Comedy Scientist." You could even change your name altogether, creating a stage name or a nom de plume. This is commonplace in Hollywood; actors and actresses do it all the time. Albert Brooks was born Albert Einstein. David Bowie was born David Robert Jones. Joan Rivers was Joan Alexandra Melinsky. Carey Grant was Archibald Leach. Michael Keaton was Michael John Douglas. Katie Perry was Katherine Elizabeth Hudson. The list goes on and on. Some of these people might have changed their name legally, but a lot didn't; they just had to differentiate themselves professionally.

Next, consider the impression your brand leaves on people. The impression you leave should be connected to your bigger vision. Authenticity is key. Part of the impression you leave should be connected to your story and what you've had to overcome. When someone reads or hears your name, they should feel something.

ABA–Always Be Authentic

I can't overemphasize the importance of authenticity. People will eventually see through you if you aren't authentic. In addition, not being authentic is exhausting! Always be your true self. Anything less will shine through your content, and your audience will lose trust.

My mantra in everything is "walk the talk," and I always strive to live by that. There are some speakers who don't. For instance, some speakers talk about preventive medicine, but are significantly overweight. Who is going to trust them? They aren't walking the talk. Don't tell people you are an expert or knowledgeable about something. Show them.

Finally, how can you stand out while still being identified within a particular vertical? Establish a unique focus within your vertical that proves to your audience or paying clients that you are uniquely valuable, but also trustworthy.

What is your fundamental truth others don't believe?

This is a key concept to becoming a successful thought leader. Your content differentiator is your fundamental truth that most others don't believe. In some cases, they aren't even aware of this truth. It is that thing you know in your heart to be true that goes against the norm.

For example, my fundamental truth with first book, *The Patient as CEO,* is that patients are the CEO of the healthcare team. Until recently, the entire medical community did not believe that, and a lot still don't. With this TLF book and platform, my fundamental belief or truth is that 90 percent of people have the potential to be a thought leader if they only have and follow the right formula.

Your unique position signals to your audience that you understand them and can provide them with solutions. Again, trust is key. People search the internet every day for answers, and if your content provides some answers, you build trust.

A Strong Brand Inspires

Your unique perspective and opinion is your personal brand. A strong brand creates demand for your products and services. People buy better versions of themselves, so inspiration is the name of the game. Position your brand in a way that is inspirational and will help others become better at whatever they wish to achieve. Take this very book as an example. It is a guide to help people fulfill their own potential.

> **Inspire people to become better versions of themselves.**

Consider the Pepsi story of the 60s. Coke was beating Pepsi by a significant amount, so Pepsi decided on a new way to market. Instead of focusing on the product, they focused on the image of people who drink Pepsi, coming up with the "Pepsi Generation." They tied a drink to an inspirational concept. They focused on who you would be if you drank Pepsi—the freedom you would feel—and that drew people in.

Apple knows a thing or two about branding as well. Their whole platform is based on "think different." They inspire people not with the product features, but with a feeling—who you will be if you use the products.

Branding used to focus much more on how a product would "fix the problem." Today, people need to feel inspired and emotionally connected.

I shared previously that my life goal is to impact one hundred million patients worldwide. My drive behind that life goal is directly tied to my experience of spending much of my life being sick. I want to keep others from having to endure that kind of pain, in addition to paying back the world of healthcare: the doctors, the professionals, and nurses who took care of me. I want to make a huge impact on the world of medicine. When I speak or write, the emotions connected to my story come through. Those emotions are central to my brand.

Your brand needs a backbone. Once you've identified your fundamental truth, tie that with your *why*, that thing or experience that drives you. What are you passionate about? What is your personal story? Your entire platform could be built around the success of beating the odds or turning a loss into opportunity.

Elements of Your Personal Brand

In order to have a strong personal brand, you must have the essential elements in place. You've started with a bold vision based on your *why* and now you want to share who you are and what you do with the world.

Photo

The first basic element of your personal brand is a clean, crisp, full-face photo of yourself. Make your photo consistent across your website and social media channels so people easily recognize you. Using a clean white or colored background will allow you to stand out on websites. I prefer white, as it blends into most websites well. A recognizable photo is so important because we remember things after repeated exposure. This will be the one photo you can consistently send to all conferences and websites when you first start your thought leadership journey. Further into your career, you can mix it up, but when you first start, you want people to recognize you immediately.

While I recommend getting a professional photo done, start where you can. Today, you can even use a smartphone camera and get a high-resolution photo. As with everything in this process, don't wait until the ideal conditions, because they will never come. Anything delayed puts you farther from your goal.

A signature look is important, as it adds to your being easily recognizable. Your signature look must be authentic. A forced costume or look will make you feel uncomfortable, and that will come across in person and on stage. You could differentiate yourself easily by adding in a scarf, fun bowtie, or uniquely framed glasses. Incorporate those tweaks into your photo and whenever you are on stage. Maybe you always wear a red dress, distinctive jeans, or a hoodie sweatshirt. A unique hairstyle, a formal pinstriped suit, or unusual and visible shoes can also add to a signature look. The key is that these elements are used consistently. One thing to note: if you are connected with a corporation, make sure your look conforms to that corporate culture.

My signature look is connected to my curly mass of blonde hair, but it also includes everything from my shoes to choice of dress. If you are unsure about the aspect of yourself that stands out the most, ask your friends, or consider how you would look as a caricature. You might even have someone do a caricature of you. What stands out? Take that aspect of yourself and accentuate it.

Stereotypically, people think you can either look smart or good, but not both. I disagree with that mentality. One has nothing whatsoever to do with the other;

it's like comparing apples to yachts. You don't have to choose between being smart or looking good. When I was first starting out, the advice I was given by professional speakers was to not wear makeup, pull my hair back, and instead of dresses, wear jeans and flats. They said that was the way people would take me seriously. I have proven that advice to be incorrect by not following it, and I want to make sure others don't alter their authentic selves because of a false stereotype.

For further inspiration on honing your signature look while being authentic, you can hire a stylist for one or two sessions. They may come up with ideas that never crossed your mind, but may be a great, comfortable, and authentic look for you. The stylist may come up with that one small tweak. For women, creating a signature look is typically easier because we have more accoutrements to play with than men.

When working with men on their signature look, I've noticed most gravitate immediately to the pocket square as their differentiator. Pocket squares are awesome and look great. Unfortunately, it's not enough of a differentiator in and of itself. Instead, consider using it as an addition to add extra oomph to an already great look. The pocket square alone isn't going to stand out in headshots, as most headshots won't even include the pocket. Secondly, it's a small detail that can be seen and appreciated up close, but not on stage or in a large crowd. Whatever you choose to use as your signature look, be sure it's obvious.

Tagline

A tagline is a reiterated phrase identified with an individual, group, or product. It is also known as a slogan.

The tagline I developed for my first platform was this: *how technology empowers the healthcare consumer.* What is a tagline that sums up your personal brand? This will be part of your long and short bios and any presentation you do.

Think of your tagline as your thesis. When you have it, you don't need to write your elevator pitch and bios yourself. You can work with companies that specialize in copy, freelance writers, or a PR company to develop those from your tagline.

Expanding Your Number of Catchphrases

What is your signature catchphrase you could write on the back of a napkin? This should quickly describe different areas of your expertise.

When creating my first platform on patient empowerment and technology disrupting medicine, I thought like a company branding department, and brainstormed fifteen to twenty catchphrases. One catchphrase was "The Patient as CEO," which later became the title of my book. Other ones included "Doctors as Medical Engineers," "The Era of the Patient," "Wearable Technology Creating an Internet of You," and "Diagnostics on Demand." I actually trademarked a couple of these phrases. Your catchphrases need to be new, unique, and memorable. While you may or may not take the steps to actually trademark your catchphrase, the process of creating them is still important.

Once you create your catchphrases, you need to use them frequently, so that people associate those concepts with you. For the first year of the patient empowerment and technology disrupting medicine platform, I tested all the different catchphrases out to see how people responded to them. The ones I still use today are the ones people reacted to. You also need to love your catchphrases. If you don't, repeating them hundreds or thousands of times will be torturous.

Once you have your tagline and catchphrases, then it's time to market and use them. One of the best ways to do this is to create social media banners.

Hire a graphic designer or even use one of the many free tools available to quickly create these. You could use software like Canva—basically a drag and drop design software for beginner designers. I used my life goal—*working to impact one hundred million patients worldwide*—as a catchphrase on my LinkedIn header banner. This is a small step you can take that will significantly build your branding.

Bio

Next, you need to develop a short, medium, and long bio. You need to have these on-demand, so you can copy and paste them as needed. These can especially come in handy when someone needs to introduce you, as your short bio can double as a stage or email introduction.

Your short bio should be between seventy and one hundred words. Your medium bio should be between one hundred and 200. Your long should bio be between 200 and 400. Each should tell the story of you, and they should be easy to skim through, with keywords that stand out. Everything, even in your long bio, should be relevant. Every word should refer back to your central brand. Keep in mind that it is not the date range that makes something relevant in a bio; it is the relevance to your brand.

Your bio tells the story of you.

If you want to write your bios yourself, you can always Google others' bios or download a template to work from. A bio will typically include your name, your professional experience, your education experience (if relevant), your current title, your company title, and any publications or awards you have.

Marketing companies, PR companies, and professional editors can help you write your bio. The reason to bring on help, at least initially, is that you are sometimes too close to the content, since it's about you. A good expert can take one look at your platform ideas and LinkedIn profile, have a quick chat with you, and come back with a great bio. Once you have a solid template bio, you can tweak and update going forward. Initially, I had Influence & Co. write my first long bio, specifically targeted to launch me as a thought leader. Once I had that template in place, I was able to update it and edit it going forward.

Here is a list of aspects to include in your bio:

- [NAME] is a [PROFESSION]

- Drive or skill

- Current title and company

- Relevant past titles and companies (this gets cut down for the short bio)

- Relevant education

- Any major publications or articles

- Any major accolades (awarded #1, or grew the last business to $X, or was a finalist in something prestigious)

If you need to condense your bio, consider what elements that take up the most room. If half of your bio is about your publications, then maybe it would be beneficial for you to simply title yourself as an author and give the high-level view: "over 50 publications, including X-Magazine and X-Newspaper." In your long bio, you can be more detailed. If you have done something prestigious or been awarded in some significant way, make that your last line. Your educational credentials, once a requirement for bios, are no longer needed. If your educational background is relevant for your platform, go ahead and include it. If it's not a relevant fact, or is already understood without listing it, then don't feel like you need to include education at all. For example, if someone has an MD in their title, or mentions the word "physician" in their bio, the audience already understands they went to medical school. That said, you might want to include specifics, especially if you went to a top school.

When it comes to bios for programs and websites, you want to do your best to match the length of others' bios. That way, you don't have to worry about the conference or editor editing it down and cutting out something you wanted people to see and notice. Sometimes, when I am unsure of how long my bio can be, I send the editor a couple of lengths. The editor can use any of those options, making it more likely that the reader will see what I want them to see. With all elements of your brand, you want to be in total control. Using templated language of different lengths helps you stay in control of this element.

Your bio is another place where you can repackage, copy, and paste. People will start asking how to introduce you on stage, and you will need to have an answer prepared. You may go with a simple one-liner, so you can get straight into telling your story at the beginning of your keynote. Some speakers have a two- to three-sentence introduction that proves their credibility as it relates to the content they are about to present. Whatever you do, give the presenter something different than a list of accomplishments, because the audience will zone out if they hear that.

They likely have easy access to your bio on the website and program if they want to know more about you.

Instead, provide the moderator with something that will get the audience's attention. The most important aspect of a keynote is that it's being given by you. You don't want a stranger stumbling through one or two dry paragraphs about you. Unless the moderator is high personality, that will only bring down the energy in the room.

You want to also become familiar with your bios, so you can quickly introduce yourself. If you are networking, being able to introduce yourself with your tagline right off the bat will help get the conversation going quicker. Make your intro short, peppy, and interesting—something that encapsulates who you are in ten to twenty seconds. Then practice, practice, practice. The key is that you don't drone on and on because you'll lose people's attentions, and they may only remember that you were boring, not the content of what you said, which is the important thing. People remember how you make them feel, not what you said. We'll discuss this more in Chapter 7, when we talk about in-person networking.

As with everything you write, from your bio to your book, simplify it to the least number of words possible. When writing articles or creating keynote slides or scripts, you always want to go back and take out as many words as possible and drop unnecessary details. Here again, you want to ask, "Can this be tighter?"

Personal Elevator Pitch

According to Wikipedia, an elevator pitch is "a short description of an idea, product, company, or oneself that explains the concept in a way such that any listener can understand it in a short period of time." For a personal elevator pitch, the description generally "explains one's skills and goals." The goal is simply to convey an overall concept in an exciting way. Unlike a sales pitch, there may not be a clear buyer/seller relationship present.

When crafting your elevator pitch, consider the transformation you are offering. People don't buy products; they buy better versions of themselves. Inspiration is the name of the game. How can you position your brand so that it is inspirational, and will help people become better at whatever they want to do? For example, I am using this book as a guide to help people fulfill their own potential.

Also consider your fundamental truth that others don't believe. What is that thing you know is true, but most people don't know about, or it isn't a widely spread belief? With my patient as CEO vertical, my fundamental truth is that most people don't know patients should be in control of their health and care. For the TLF, it is the fact that anyone, *anyone* can be a thought leader if they put in the hard work, strategy, and capital (i.e., follow the right formula). Some people think of thought leadership as "being discovered" like an actor or musician, rather than building it like a business with a strategy and brand. My goal is to help other see what it actually takes to be called a thought leader, and that is part of the elevator pitch I give when I talk about the TLF platform.

Workbook Action Steps

In Chapter 1, we discussed mapping out your overarching goal and your mission. We discussed what drove you toward that goal or your *why*. Why do you get out of bed every day? What in your life has happened that brought you onto this path? I want you to consider those same questions again. Write down the ways you plan to walk the talk. If you are someone passionate about wearable devices, then you should probably wear one, right? Walk the talk and ABA—Always Be Authentic.

It's time to brainstorm about your branding. Jot down ideas as you go through the list below:

1. Part 1: Components of your brand

    a. What's your fundamental truth, something you believe that others might not also believe?

    b. How do you "walk the talk"?

    c. What gives rise to your credibility? This can be education, previous experience, affiliations, or even a single event.

2. Part 2: Expression of your brand

    a. New headshot photo: make sure it is high resolution, full face, has a solid background color, great lighting, and only includes you in your signature look.

    b. Set a timer for five minutes, then brainstorm to generate notes for each of these four other major elements of your brand (total time: twenty minutes):

        1. Tagline

2. Ten to twenty catchphrases, knowing you won't use them all

3. Two or three bio lengths. One way is to start this action item is to write a long bio that includes everything about you, and then edit down by cutting out nonrelevant facts, and grouping things like achievements, publications, or experience. Here, you can also start to create your in-person spoken introduction and stage introduction, both subsets of that long bio.

4) Elevator pitch

3. Part 3: Put your branding into action

a. Create (or hire someone to create) social media banners and posts that will highlight your goal, tagline, fundamental truth, or some of your catchphrases.

b. Optional: Hire a company or consultant to help you craft your bios. If you go this route, then actually take a step. The easiest place to start is with a copywriting platform like Scripted. If you don't like the result, hire someone else!

Chapter 6

· · · · · · · · ·   · · · · · · · · ·

Content, Content, Content

In order to build out your content channels, you have to first have the foundation in place. As we discussed in Chapter 4, you need to develop your initial content catalog. Make sure you love this foundational content—enough to write and talk about it for the next five to ten years. Like popular musicians perform the same songs over and over, you have to commit to your content for the long term.

You also need to believe 100 percent in your foundational content. If you don't, you won't come across as authentic. You're not selling an app. You're not simply thinking about what you can monetize. You're sharing knowledge that is aligned to you—your beliefs, your truth, and your experience.

Those who build a large following with their content are the ones who don't give up. Consistency is the key. I helped run a healthcare blog in 2010. We published a new article each weekday, and always had a two-week queue of articles ready to go. Even with this kind of consistency, it took years to build a substantial following. With podcasts, most people give up after about a year. Success is cumulative, and if you give up after only one year, you will think you can never win. Keep with things long enough, and you'll hit an inflection point and suddenly grow considerably more quickly.

Keep in mind that your follower's engagement with your content is more important than the number of followers you have. So, when thinking about a "substantial following," substantial here refers to the number of followers who are actually interested and engaging with your ideas. Engaged followers more easily become customers. A smaller number of engaged followers who convert to some form of a sale are much better than a large number of followers who aren't interested enough in your content to convert through one of your defined revenue streams.

The Landscape of Building Content

Today, it's not easy to make money being only a journalist or author; the competition for those few paid spots is significant and fierce. Publishers only ever have a few open spots for new authors. Newspapers and online platforms only hire so many journalists. Hard copy magazines can only use a handful of writers.

You must approach content your own way. You can publish a lot of your content for free, charge people individually with a membership model or one-time purchase (as with books), or pay-to-play, where you pay to publish content in a highly visible location.

When you first launch yourself as a thought leader, you must find ways to publish your written content. The benefit of this new publishing landscape is that you can have full ownership of your content. You have total control over your messaging and your brand, which is important if your revenue model isn't only based on books or writing. When a publisher, newspaper, or magazine pays you for your content, they have a say in your content, because their revenue stream comes from selling and packaging that specific content. Their preferences might keep you from achieving your long-term goals or succeeding with revenue streams that are significantly larger than book sales or payment for articles.

Start thinking of each content channel as a lever to open doors to new opportunities. The good news is that once your content catalog is in place, you can reuse your content by repackaging and repurposing it. It doesn't matter whether you build a following with podcasts, video, or a blog; the same content can be used over and over again in different forms, which we'll explore later in this chapter.

Audience and Channels

Many books focus on how to reach your audience through particular content channels. The truth is that the channels themselves are always shifting. At the time of writing this book, videos and photos are hot. Over the next five years, we will likely see more augmented, virtual, and mixed-reality platforms. Social media platforms also regularly change their algorithms, which affects what they promote, and which channels might be most useful to you.

The key is to know where your audience is now. If you aren't using any social media content channels yet, that's okay. Take some time to think about what type of content your dream audience would consume. Do they like things in video form? Do they like to download podcasts or listen to audiobooks while driving? Do they like Twitter? Do they read a lot of trade-specific journals? What content channels are they using?

To understand that dream audience, it's helpful to create customer avatars or profiles that will translate and convert to your revenue streams. Who do you need to reach for your thought leader business model, *You, Inc.,* to be successful? Consider these questions to build your avatar: What is their job and education level? What generation are they in? Do they have children, and what ages are their children? Are they married, divorced, widowed, single, with a life partner, or in a long-term relationship? Are they in debt, avid investors, affluent, middle or low income? What are their goals or motivations? The more detail you have around your top five to ten customer profiles, the better. Once you start understanding who these people are and what their lives are like, you can have a better idea of what channels they might be using. At the same time, you will understand what messaging will speak to them.

You can also think about audience as primary and secondary. Your primary audience consists of those who will pay you for something, money that actually converts to your revenue streams. Your secondary audience consists of those who influence the people who pay you. Your secondary audience might be your primary audience's boss, spouse, children, colleagues, friends, educators, doctors, accountants, or lawyers. When you influence the secondary audience, they can potentially influence your primary audience through referrals.

Also consider what channels you like to use. In this way, you can keep designing your entire world. What do you love to do? If you hate Twitter, you should not be on Twitter. If it's an important channel for your audience, and you really need to be on that platform, hire someone to manage it for you. If you love to create video, you have a lot of choices, from YouTube, Instagram, Facebook, and Vimeo, to name a handful. Find those places where you and your audience intersect.

Whenever posting, make sure there is a photo that populates the post, as photos get a lot more attention than just text. I am typically active on three to four platforms, and those platforms will likely shift over the next few years to augmented, mixed, or virtual reality. Currently, I'm on Facebook and Instagram to share happenings in my life and career, whereas LinkedIn and Twitter are dedicated to my thought leadership content, without any of my personal life included.

Publishing

When you are considering content, you are likely thinking about the possibility of a book. As a thought leader, should you write a book?

The short answer is *Yes*.

The long answer is *Absolutely*!

In today's business climate, you need both your LinkedIn URL and also an Amazon URL with your book or books. Writing a book was the single biggest catalyst in my becoming a thought leader and professional speaker, but only because I had set up a solid platform before launching it. Think of a book as a $3 business card. The point is not primarily to make book sales; you care about the credibility a book gives you. An at-cost paperback copy of your book will likely cost you just a few dollars. Just as you would with business cards, you want to keep a box of fifty books to hand out to people at any time.

A book is just a $3 business card.

The good news is that you have many options for how to go about writing and publishing your first book. This doesn't have to be scary or intimidating. There are many hacks you can use.

The traditional publishing route is an option, but I don't recommend it for first-time or unknown authors. If you want to go this route but don't have any following, you'll have a difficult time getting an agent or in the front door of a traditional publishing house. To get signed by a publishing house and get a big advance, you need to already be a well-known expert or have a massive, engaged following ready to buy your book. Think celebrities, politicians, and CEOs of publicly traded companies. If you sign with a traditional publisher, and this is your first book, expect little to no advance fee.

Going this route, you also typically need to have an agent. When you fill out an agent form, it seems all they care about is your ability to get the book into the perfect format, with a perfectly written thesis. I can't possibly go with an agent who is more worried about my ability to format my content into their rigid forms then my actual content and marketability. Furthermore, a traditional publishing house with standard contracts ultimately control your content. You will have a difficult time pulling out some of the content from the book and repurposing it into articles, online video programs, keynotes, workshops, and events. This is obviously an issue for thought leaders, who have many revenue streams.

What agents will do is shop your book around for you, and that could be helpful for the right person, such as a CEO of major company or a well-known investor. They might gain added credibility and reach more people by getting on TV or getting on the *NY Times* Best Seller List without having to hack the system (more on that later). Going with a traditional publishing house can potentially get you into brick and mortar stores and libraries as well, whereas self-publishing does not. That said, I haven't bought a book in a brick and mortar for over fifteen years. With all of retail going digital, it's hard to imagine having your book in a store or library is going to be a perk for much longer.

As a thought leader, you want to use your book as a lever to open doors. A traditional publishing house only concentrates on book sales, because that's their main revenue stream. When you are looking at $10,000 for one speaking gig, you're not as concerned with a few dollars profit per copy of your book. You're concerned with having a quality book that shares your message with your voice, and that you can use to build your credibility. That, in turn, is what feeds your main revenue streams.

Go the PDF Route

One option for a first-time author without a substantial following would be to simply go the self-publishing route. It's the fastest and easiest route if you're self-directed and know how to take care of your own cover and formatting. I would recommend you outsource those elements to a designer or virtual assistant with experience. If you outsource a lot of the little tasks required, all you have to do is write up as little as twenty pages, get it formatted, turn the document into a PDF, and upload it to Amazon. You could sell this little book for whatever price you choose: $0.99 to $30 or more, depending on how valuable it is to your audience.

Of course, writing even twenty pages of a book can be hard if you don't have a lot of experience with this form of writing. It might even produce a lot of anxiety. It's important to remember that the first steps are the hardest. You're not alone if you have a hard time writing a book; many people find it difficult. Now that I've been doing it for years, I actually love writing, and I even enjoy the editing process. However, I definitely didn't start out loving this process a few years ago.

With all the obstacles you might face around writing, you can hack it even further. Hire on-demand writers through Scripted or any of the other writers-on-demand platforms to write ten to twenty articles around your subject matter. Then either write an opening and closing that stiches the articles together or outsource those transitions to an on-demand writer. Suddenly, you have a sixty-page book. For this hack to be successful, you need to make sure to give the writers clear instructions and samples of your writing. Otherwise it won't match your voice or content portfolio. A book can't be thrown away like an article can be. Only use this option if you know your content backwards and forwards already. You will still need to be able to deliver flawless presentations and answer Q&As about your content on stage, in podcasts, and during interviews.

With *The Patient as CEO,* I used a new category in publishing services—Lioncrest Publishing through Scribe Media. With *The Thought Leader Formula,* I went with a traditional publisher—Indigo River Publishing—who allowed me to keep my intellectual property (IP). The reason I went with the traditional publisher the second time around was because I love working with young companies, full of entrepreneurs. A traditional publisher does take a percentage split of the profits, but that also means they have a vested interest in helping me succeed.

For both books, I used Scribe Media services. Scribe Media is a company that helps you write your book more expediently and professionally, while still allowing you to maintain all ownership of the ideas and content.

With Scribe Media, you work on outlining first. They are experts at extracting the right information from your brain, and organizing that content into an extremely detailed, professional outline. This takes only a few phone calls. Then you have another three to six phone calls with your "scribe," where you dive into the details of the content, methodically following the outline. The calls are all recorded and transcribed, so you are basically talking your entire book. They take that transcription and edit it into a book.

A couple editing rounds later, your book is finished, and then they take care of all the remaining details after receiving your input: cover design, Amazon profile, formatting for paperback, hardcover, e-book. You can even have them do an audiobook version for you.

To be clear, the book is 100 percent your words and ideas. They don't fact check, or research (unless you pay an additional fee). They are not ghostwriters. The book is all you, in your voice, with your tone and phrasing. Of course, you can always go with a standard ghostwriter, but I wouldn't recommend that route unless you can afford a top one, who charges $100,000 or more. Ghostwriters are independent consultants, and their abilities vary all over the board.

There are other companies using similar processes to Scribe Media, designed to capture and package your ideas, voice, and material. This is a fantastic option for those who like systems and working with people to get something completed; it gets the job done in around six months, as long as you stick to the schedule and put in the work required.

Even though I used Scribe Media's system, I approached the two books—this one you're reading and *The Patient as CEO*—very differently. *The Patient as CEO* required significant research. I interviewed entrepreneurs, scientists, patients, healthcare professionals, and more. I also did a lot of my own research online. For the three months leading up to starting the book, I read technology and medical publications for two to three hours a day. I pasted entire articles into a Word doc. I then divided the Word doc by chapters, which I had already outlined. Each chapter focused on one technology: sensors, artificial intelligence, 3D printing, robotics, etc. After the article was pasted under the correct chapter (including the URL), I would highlight in yellow the paragraph or two that encapsulated the concept I wanted to add to the book. By the time I started the phone recordings, I had all the research and backing content gathered. On the recorded calls, I would scroll through the docs and look for the highlighted sections to remind myself of the concepts to discuss.

I approached The Thought Leader Formula very differently. Before starting the recorded calls, I had already written 20,000 words of the 40,000 words I was shooting for with this book. Since this book is essentially my personal project plan to become a speaker, combined with years and years of education and work experience in this industry, it required a lot less effort, research, and fact checking. I've been living and breathing events, entrepreneurship, and the speaking world for my entire career. I just had to get all that info out of my head, and into a well-organized package.

The Cover

Living in a digital world, fewer people will likely hold your physical book in their hands. Even fewer will click to buy. Still fewer will actually read your book. These are the realities.

While many people won't hold your book or even read it, what many people *will* see is your book cover image—in all your marketing, on social media, in every email. Because the cover is so important, it needs to get your entire platform across in a memorable way. If people buy the book, that's great, but what's more important is that you are building your brand.

Here is a breakdown of the strategic cover design for my first book, *The Patient as CEO: How Technology Empowers the Healthcare Consumer:*

- A strong title: *The Patient as CEO* is very obviously about healthcare and patient empowerment.

  O Not too clever or obtuse

  O Should sum up your platform (think back to the napkin method)

- A strong subtitle (or tagline)

  O Tells the deeper story about the content of the book (often includes an interesting point that makes the viewer consider what's inside)

- Endorsement and credibility quotes

  ○ The quote on my cover reads, "A must read for patients to understand the current medical revolution driven by accelerating technology." It is signed by an MD, which also gave me credibility.

- A strong photo

  ○ Remember, you are selling you, not the book.

  ○ Through this photo, you can impart subtle messages that will be remembered.

  ○ For the photo on my first book, I wore a white dress. The subtle message I was sharing was that as a healthcare consumer, I am part of the healthcare team, as doctors wear white coats, nurses stereotypically wear all white (though not in practice anymore).

Let's examine these points a bit further.

First, you need to make the title clear and concise. I've seen book titles where the author was trying to be clever or obtuse, and it doesn't work well. People will potentially remember the title, but they will have no idea what it's about or how it connects to the author's platform. They often don't have the time, desire, or attention to click through and figure out what the book is going to teach them. Make it effortless for people to understand the focus of the book, which should be directly connected to your entire platform. What are your three or four words that sum up the main theme? If you have someone's attention for one second, will they remember you and associate you with your subject matter expertise?

Then, with your subtitle, expand a bit so that viewers can understand a little more about your unique angle or perspective. For my first book, I focused on getting value from every word of the subtitle, *How Technology Empowers the Healthcare Consumer*. The subtitle tells a whole story that reinforces the main title. It described how patients can become CEOs, specifically by using technology that empowers them. The term "healthcare consumer" redefined patients as the customer with buying power and choice—a concept that was unheard of in healthcare until recently. I put deep thought into each word of my subtitle.

I have also found it useful to showcase endorsements and credibility quotes on your cover. I chose a well-known thought leader in technology to write the endorsing quote on my front cover. The way the quote was worded was strategic as well, and I worked with Peter Diamandis, the MD who wrote the endorsing quote, closely to have his quote reinforce the title. The best way to get highly relevant quotes from extremely busy people is to help them by sending suggestions. I have pages of quotes from top thought leaders. Most wrote their own. For a few, I sent over suggestions written in their voice, using phrasing I had heard them use many times. The quote on my first cover described my entire book, but also bolstered my credibility.

A photo of yourself can go a long way. Remember, at the end of the day you are selling you, not a book. I'm not flexible about taking myself off the cover. I strategically figured out what to wear, knowing it would help convey my point. I wore a white dress, because in the world of healthcare doctors and nurses both wear white. I wanted to appear as part of the team. It reinforced my platform while getting my face out there. Since your book cover populates every article or social media post, it's your face plus your back-of-the-napkin platform description (title, subtitle, and quote) that people actually see.

Becoming a Best Seller

If you are going the self-publishing route, you are most likely not going to get on the New York Times Best Seller's list. In the business category, it's extremely difficult to get on that list, period. Some of those who do sometimes game the system spend around $100,000 to upwards of $150,000 to buy a certain number of books in certain areas. There are companies you can hire that will help you get on this list by strategically having contacts buy the right number of books at the right time, in the right place.

In the world of Amazon, it's much easier to become a best seller using that route. You can tag yourself with industry-specific keywords, which makes your book easier to find. Within two days of release, *The Patient as CEO* became a number one best seller in biotechnology. Of course, this was supported by a lot of marketing around the book, specifically targeting a big email list I had and using a marketing company and a PR company to make a big splash on the launch. A professional speaker friend, Brian Rashid, also published an article on the book in his *Forbes* column on the day of the release, increasing the book's marketing reach.

If you're a first-time author, focus on your Amazon rankings. Don't be concerned about becoming a

New York Times best seller. A lot of it is vanity. You're creating a robust platform as a thought leader, you don't need that extra seal of approval. Those of us inside the industry know it's gamed anyway. When we see *The New York Times* Best Seller List, it doesn't impress us. Rather than spending all that money to game the system, I would rather invest in startups. You can reference commentary on this from best-selling author, Tucker Max.[3]

Other Avenues

A few other content channels could be helpful to build and maintain for your overall platform. Some thought leaders have their own blog where they consistently publish content. This can act as the hub for your content catalog and ongoing articles or videos. When you share your content to social media channels, you will often be sharing from your blog. This means that those who click on your links will find their way to your main website, where they might sign up for your email newsletter, reach out and contact you, or even buy one of your products.

---

[3] Tucker Max, "How to Get a Book Published and Choose the Right Publishing Option," Scribe Writing, November 15, 2018. https://scribewriting.com/book-publishing-options/.

Other content channel options include online magazines, industry-specific publications, and LinkedIn. A lot of my content has been shared in *Becker's Hospital Journal* or *Frost and Sullivan,* because they were relevant to my particular vertical and the audience I wanted to reach at the time. LinkedIn is a fantastic place to publish or republish your articles as well, and I recommend you have a significant amount of your content housed there. When people read your article on LinkedIn, they are more likely to visit to your profile and see information about you right then and there. The opposite is also true: when people look at your LinkedIn profile, all your articles are right there for them to read. The more people read about your experience and credentials, the more you will build your credibility.

Finally, you may consider venturing into the world of podcasts to share your content. Podcasts are on the rise, some of them now being funded by venture companies. They've been around since 2000, but until recently you couldn't easily track user behavior like you can with websites. As of December 2017, Apple, a longtime podcast distributor, rolled out podcast episode analytics. With this change, podcast producers can see how their listeners are engaging and respond in turn. You could get a podcast funded, or you could use it as a way to seamlessly drive traffic to your higher ticket items.

Workbook Action Steps

Now it's time to start putting this advice into action. How can you begin to create and distribute your ideas through different forms of content? Use the following action steps to get started.

Pretend you are writing a book. Outline the following:

1. What's the title—the three or four words that sum up the main theme of your platform?

2. Write the subtitle; this should expand and reinforce the title in six or seven words.

3. Write the ideal quote on the front cover, including who might be a great option to write that quote. The type of phrases you can include that work well: "must read," "fascinating book," "page turner," "invaluable guidance," "filled with," "inspiring," "enthralling," "compelling," "brilliant," "if you X, then buy this book," "clear," "realistic," "provocative."

4. What are you wearing and doing in the photo on the cover? What does the background look like? Is it a plain color background, or is there scenery? If the book is about tennis, for example, you might include a racket, ball, or

court in the picture.

Now take some time to define your market so you can choose the right content channels.

5. To begin, outline three avatars of the type of people that you're trying to reach. You might have a lot more than that, but one point of the TLF system is that you actually DO it. Starting with three quick ones means you took action and another step forward to achieving your goals. For each avatar, consider the following:

    a. Age and generation

    b. Gender

    c. Job

    d. Industry

    e. Education

    f. Location

    g. Marital status

    h. Children

    i. Health

j.   Interests or hobbies

k.   Values

l.   What social media channels do they like?

m. What type of content do they like to consume (audiobooks, podcasts, video, articles, memes, pictures, inspirational quotes, traditional periodicals, or even newspapers)?

6. Now outline what you like to do, and already use: What distribution channels do you enjoy (LinkedIn, Instagram, Twitter, YouTube, etc.)? How do you like to create content (record videos, write articles, tweet, photos, etc.)?

7. Now compare. Where do you and your avatars intersect? Choose one to three channels to focus on, at least initially.

Chapter 7

· · · · · · · · · ●   ● · · · · · · · ·

Networking Ninja

One of the most important aspects of networking is building relationships before you need them. You can't just briefly meet someone, and then pounce on them with an ask. Having relationships in place months or years before you need them is crucial. The more relationships you have, the more opportunities you will have.

In your initial networking, be authentic. Don't force connections or make it all about you. Instead, remember that giving is much better than receiving. The more people you help, the more it will come back to you in unexpected ways.

Start by Volunteering

My best advice and hack to start networking? Volunteer, volunteer, volunteer. Look for events in your space and apply to volunteer. The best positions are working the registration table or being the speaker manager or the stage manager. The easiest way to get a volunteer position is to find contact info on the event website, and just email the people running the event. Offer your services for free and tell them why you think their event is worth your volunteer time. Focus on why you think their event is great and how you can help them achieve their goals. If you can get a direct introduction from one of your contacts to someone on the event team, that's even better. Another way to get in the door is to first attend an event as a paying attendee and make it a point to interact with everyone on the event team. Now you'll have those relationships in place and can volunteer your time for their next event.

One bonus when volunteering for an event is, you never have those awkward times during an event when you aren't interacting with anyone and aren't sure who to approach to interact with next. Everyone, even an extrovert, has those periods of time at an event when they are alone, between conversations, and suddenly feeling anxious because they are alone.

That's normal, and few escape that feeling. When you are on the event team, even as a volunteer, you always have something to do or someone to interact with.

If you only have a little time to volunteer, ask to work the registration table, as you can show up at the event less than an hour before it begins, and your job is usually done by about an hour into the event, assuming the number of late stragglers taper off by then. You will be the first person many, if not all, attendees will see and meet. In fact, for events of 250 or less, this is the only person that gets to meet everyone! If you were to attend as a regular attendee, you only have time to meet a handful of people. Another major benefit is that you can also take a photo of the attendee list to follow up with everyone on LinkedIn when you get home.

Another great position that will require more of your time is the speaker manager position. As a volunteer (versus an employee, who would have a greater number of tasks and responsibility), you would help coordinate the speakers before the event with the basics, like logistics or getting their slides for the AV team. Because you are interacting with the speakers both before and during the event, you can build a relationship with them, and they will likely remember how nice and helpful you were as a volunteer for the event. These speakers are great potential mentors, role models, colleagues, partners, co-panelists— essentially, your fellow thought leader "peeps."

Of course, you may be at a level of your career where it would seem odd for you to volunteer for check-in or speaker manager. For instance, if you're part of the C-Suite of a mature company, there are other ways to achieve similar results. If you are building thought leadership that benefits your current company, send someone from your business development or marketing department to volunteer. They can network with the company's specific goals in mind.

You can also consider being a sponsor. You don't have to spend a lot of money to be a sponsor; sometimes an in-kind donation is fine. In-kind donations can consist of marketing for the conference, media publications, donating products including wine, food, drinks, something your company makes. Even just supplying interesting, nicely done nametags is a form of sponsorship. Cash donations can range from $100 to over $3 million, depending on the conference, so you have a significant amount of wiggle room when identifying and sponsoring events. As the sponsor, you can still greet people at the entrance or registration table. You will be introduced to the speakers and have access to the greenroom (backstage speaker-ready room), especially if you ask. You can hang around the event early and late to build relationships with the entire event team. That can give you special access to things like private meeting rooms, extra parties or events before and after the conference, and the registration list. And as we'll dive into later in the book, knowing people on the event team can help you get on stage.

Another effective and strategic way to volunteer, no matter what stage of your career you are in currently, is by joining the advisory board or a committee of alumni groups, nonprofits, or local community groups that are relevant to your subject matter. You can network by being together with others in these groups. If you focus on groups that also run events, you will have a better shot at being a speaker for those events.

Approach Events Strategically

Whether you are volunteering, attending, or speaking at an event, you can still be strategic about networking. Study the speaker and attendee list in advance. In this way, you can know if attending the event is worth your time. Make a note of who you want to meet and why. It can even be helpful to have a list of the top five or ten people you want to meet pasted into a document with their photos, so you have your own pictorial project plan for the event.

Next, pull out the intro bios you created in Chapter 5 and practice. Be ready to go up to the people you want to meet and tell them why you admire them or have wanted to meet them. When I first meet someone new, I sometimes open by complimenting them on something I admire about them, but only authentically. For instance, I might say, "I read your book and it really spoke to me," or "That necklace is gorgeous", or "What you said on stage today..." If you're lying, people can tell, which is why you genuinely need to believe what you are saying. Then introduce yourself, but remember not to drone on or dominate the conversation. Use the spoken introduction you have prepared.

Bring the conversation back to them as quickly as possible. Ask them questions about themselves—especially memorable questions the person probably hasn't heard before. If the person hears "What's an interesting book your read this year?" instead of "Where are you from?" they might be more engaged in the conversation. By keeping them on their toes, you get to know them more quickly. You'll see their real personalities come out.

At conferences, the best times to network are during the meals and breaks. I always eat before each meal or break, so I don't have to stand in line at the food table or at the bar. I also don't want to have my mouth full of food, trying to answer questions. In addition, if you're starving during networking time, your biggest focus will be on the food, which is NOT the reason you are there. Breaks and meals are the prime networking times during events. If you are too hungry, you won't be thinking as clearly, won't be as articulate, and you might even appear uninterested or anxious. If you can't get food before the breaks or meals, bring a protein shake or bar with you. When I speak at events, I usually just go up to the wait staff (or event team) twenty minutes before the meal and ask for access to the food then. After explaining I am a speaker, they always say yes.

Whether you are a speaker or attendee, find some people from the conference and say, "Hey, let's all go out tonight for a drink." That way, you can continue the networking on a deeper level and build the relationships with these new contacts. Shared experience is a great way to bond with people.

As with everything you do, lead with value. Most people love to have photos of themselves on stage that they can post to social media the same day. If you're in the audience, grab some great photos of the person on stage, and either post to social media yourself, or find them after they get offstage and transfer the photos to them via Apple airdrop, text, or email. If you have their contact info already, send them the photos right when you take them. I make a point to always take photos of anyone I know on stage, or want to meet, and make sure to send them the photos immediately so that they can post them as soon as they get offstage. A lot of events have a professional photographer whose photos will be better than yours. However, your value add is to transfer the photos to the speaker immediately, as the pro will send them a few days or a week later. Plus, if you execute immediately, it will actually get done. The odds of your sending the photos decreases dramatically after you leave the event.

The Secret of Exclusive and Invitation-Only Events

You may want to attend or get involved with events that are "exclusive" or "by invitation only." The big secret in the world of events is that type of language is usually just marketing. If there is an application to pay for attendance, or if you need an invitation to attend before buying a ticket, that is usually just savvy sales. In the world of sales and marketing, there are some psychological hacks. Implying scarcity or exclusivity are two widely used tools to convert a potential sale to a closed sale.

The way to get around the "by invitation only" is to either have a friend who is already attending and can make an introduction for you or to find the contact info of the people running the event on the website and email them directly. Tell them why you want to attend, and how you can add value to the group. Do your homework and actually use some specific examples. If there is a cost to attend, they will probably allow you to buy a ticket. If there isn't a cost to attend, then they may invite you, depending on their goals and business model. If it's a free event to attend, someone has to foot the bill, so asking for an invitation may cost them money. At free events, they are more likely to turn you down unless you can demonstrate how you are value add and worth the cost.

Control Your Own Networking Opportunities

One option you have is to hold meetups at your house, like my friend Silvia Console Battilana and I do. Grab two or three friends as cohosts, set a theme, and have them each invite six relevant people. Suddenly, you have a top local networking event, right there in your own home!

These events are easy to run. Expert tip: with so many options, and so many people on restricted diets, food and drink can be hard. Setting expectations is the best way to counteract that. In the email invitation, make it clear what you are serving. Say "wine and cheese" or "pizza party." Don't be unclear and say something like "assorted appetizers." In that case, everyone will come to the party with different expectations. If you write "pasta dinner including meat, pesto and alfredo sauce, salad, and garlic bread" those with restrictions can plan ahead. Most people end up bringing wine. Be sure to stock up on nonalcoholic drinks and water. Too often, people running conferences and events forget to do this.

Notes on Body Language

In all in-person networking, you need to know the basics of body language. Eye contact is important. If you are looking down at your feet, others will think you're insecure or uninterested. If you're looking around the room while talking to them, they'll think you're rude or bored.

When you're talking with someone, look them in the eyes. If you happen to be waiting for someone and are keeping your eye out for them, simply say that.

You might say, "Don't mind me. I'm keeping an eye out for my business partner who's five minutes late and should be here any second." It's better to be honest so the person knows. Unless you want to ensure that a person will not follow up with you, you need to be interested in what they're saying.

If you'd like to study this area deeper, former FBI agent Joe Navarro's books and other content is one place to start your research. Here are a few other quick tips for reading body language:

- If someone has their hands crossed in front of their chest, they may be closed off, or not like what they are hearing.[4]

- If their feet are facing outwards in a V shape, they're open to you coming up and talking to them.

- If their feet are facing straight to somebody else in a group, they are likely interested in that person.

- If no one in a group has their feet in a V shape, and everyone is standing with their feet

[4] Kaplan, Michael. "Body language expert shares what signs to watch out for." New York Post. August 22, 2018. https://nypost.com/2018/08/22/body-language-expert-shares-what-signs-to-watch-out-for/.

parallel, straight toward other group members, and their upper bodies are slightly leaning in, it's a tight-knit group, and you won't be able to get in easily. You will feel like an outsider if you try to join. If you approach this type of group, you might notice that if you do get someone's attention, their hips will rotate toward you, but they won't move their feet to point at you. That means they aren't going to easily receive you into the group.

- On the flip side, watch your own body language. If I see someone standing near a group I'm in, hesitating, I step back a little, turn toward them and say, "Please, come join us." That simple invitation is a really big deal in the world of networking. Remember that the more you help others, the more it will come back to you in other ways.

Obstacles

There are several obstacles that get in the way of networking. If you are feeling awkward or scared in a room, do your best to smile and remember you have a goal. The very act of smiling can trick your brain into being happier and more relaxed.[5] It's actually a hack I use frequently to always be in a good mood. Whenever you have the opportunity to network, the point isn't to simply socialize or to see who is most popular. Your goal is to make connections and grow your network, which in turn should directly connect to your revenue sources and business model. If you think of networking as part of *You, Inc.*, you can overcome some of the obstacles you face. Still, they will exist.

Let's talk about a few.

Imposter Syndrome and FOMO

I often hear entrepreneurs talking about FOMO (the Fear of Missing Out), as well as imposter syndrome. Both have something in common: they are rooted in a lack of confidence or a lack of targeting, strategic planning, and goals. If you are fully confident in yourself and your plans, then you can take a conscious step back. You can put things into context and remind yourself why you are where you are.

I rarely if ever feel FOMO. Why? I've realized our lives are made up of a sum of our choices, and if we have

---

[5] Ruiz, Roque. "Smiling can trick your brain into happiness—and boost your health." NBC News. January 12, 2017. https://www.nbcnews.com/better/health/smiling-can-trick-your-brain-happiness-boost-your-health-ncna822591.

opportunities, it is probably because we worked to create the environment for them. For anything I've ever wanted to do, I just reversed engineered that goal to create a path I could follow to achieve it. If there is something you feel you want to be a part of, use that as a goal, reverse engineer it, and get yourself there. If you have strong foundational goals, create a road map to success, and know what you need to do to get there, then FOMO goes away.

It is frequently cited that 70 percent of people feel imposter syndrome at some point in their lives. Even lifelong learners can still suffer from imposter syndrome. Often, it's actually those who are extremely equipped and knowledgeable that still suffer from feeling like they aren't good enough, or shouldn't be able to share what they share, or charge what they charge. When you feel this happen to you, take a deep breath and remind yourself of your expertise and all the hard work you've put in. It's so easy to forget and to doubt ourselves.

I avoid feeling imposter syndrome because I am always intentional and strategic in my choices and goals. Because I have planned out my goals and the road map to them, I know every room I'm in, I've earned it. And I have the spreadsheets, documents, receipts, and completed hard work to prove it.

Chapter 7: Networking Ninja

You can avoid imposter syndrome in a similar way; strategically go after what you want. Invest time, money, and hard work to execute successfully. When you do things with intention, you know everything you've accomplished has required real effort.

Haters and Competition

One obstacle you will face is actually a simple reality: not everyone will like you. Sometimes, that's a tough pill to swallow. I can guarantee you that the more well-known you are, the more haters you will attract. They will always find ways to call you out. In fact, if some people aren't upset with you, your message may not be unique enough and you may be playing it too safe. Your fundamental truth, which we covered earlier, needs to be something you believe that others may not yet believe. If everyone agrees with you, you don't have a unique platform. Celebrate the fact that you are creating enough of an impact to have haters at all!

Unless you are generally not a good person and treat others badly, most of the time, people will dislike you because of what you do that they can see and hear. They may not even know you personally. Some that do know you personally may be haters because seeing your success or impact may bring out feelings of jealousy, unhappiness, or fear. The way a hater treats you is always a reflection of their own insecurities. Happy, secure, accomplished people don't push others down, or hate, or attack, or cause negative drama. They just don't. We know there are much better ways to spend our time than feeling negative emotions or hurting others.

There will always be room for a little, if not a lot, of drama if you let it into your life. So, don't let it in. The only thing you can do is ignore the haters and not engage with them, respond to them, or interact in any way. Know that arguing is not worth your time and walk away. That is the only way you can successfully deal with people like this. A rational conversation never convinces haters. The only thing you can control is how you react and your own emotions. You don't need to absorb their negativity; it will only bring you down. Take the high road, ignore them, and don't look back. They will eventually get tired of insulting you or thinking about you and go away.

> **Don't play their game; play yours.**

On the other hand, when thinking about potential competitors, I believe that a high tide raises all boats. There are always enough clients and customers to go around. I purposefully partner with my competitors, and together we raise each other up. Individually it's easier to fail, but together, it is easier to succeed. Competition is just market validation in the world of thought leadership. Unlike big purchases, like a car, which are made only every few years, if that, what you are selling as a thought leader is ideas, packaged up around your personality and belief system. That is 100 percent unique to you. No matter what market you're in, there is always room for a lot of thought leaders, because there is a lot of appetite for content, and as a single individual there is no way you can produce enough content to meet the daily demand of any niche. Offer to partner in some way with your competitors. If you live your life as a giver, you will get back more from the world, and sometimes in surprising ways.

Anxiety

According to CNN, an estimated 12 percent of all US adults experience social anxiety disorder at some time in their life. That means more than one out of every ten people in that room with you have had social anxiety disorder. Of course, introverts have to put in a little extra effort to overcome this anxiety.

While 12 percent experience an actual disorder, 100 percent of us feel nervous at times, especially when entering new social environments. I've heard neuroscientists theorize that throughout evolution, being accepted into a group was paramount to survival, while being cast out and alone meant death. So when entering a room where you don't know anyone and they all seem to know each other, you could be tapping into that evolutionary fear that kept your ancestors alive. If you find yourself in this situation, remind yourself of this potential theory. By assigning a reason for your nerves, you can more easily tap the nervousness down.

Wherever you fall on the spectrum when it comes to anxiety, setting simple, achievable goals can be beneficial. You don't have to build a massive network at the beginning. Set small goals that add up. If you are an introvert, plan on meeting and exchanging business cards with two people—and then you're done for that day. At your next event, aim to meet three people. At the next one, take that up to four or five. You'll feel like it's a huge win every time you achieve or surpass your goal for the day.

One great way to train yourself to be more outgoing and less shy while networking is through improv classes. Certain classes specialize in reducing social anxiety. They provide a safe, judgment-free learning experience.

One thing you learn in improv is how to be a star active listener. As an active listener, you can reflect another person's words and body language. You know how to repeat back for clarification, which helps make conversations all about the other person. Improv classes are also fantastic to train you for taking the stage and fielding Q&A, which we'll dive into in Chapter 8.

Another great tool great for both introverts and extroverts is having a wing man that you can meet or bring with you to events. The two of you support each other. I'm an extreme extrovert, but I still frequently have a networking partner in crime. My neighbor Silvia Console Battilana, who I live next door to by design, is also an extreme extrovert. We work together to network effectively, efficiently, and with the highest ROI, taking into account each other's business goals. We make a fantastic team and are better together than alone. Who in your world can you bring to your next networking opportunity?

Keep in mind that networking doesn't all have to be done in person; a lot can be accomplished online. Reply to all comments you receive, unless they're spam or unprovoked cruelty. Comment on other people's posts, articles, and videos. Share their posts, congratulate their accomplishments, and participate in discussions they begin. Interact with what they share in some way. By doing so, you can continue to network without ever leaving your computer.

Workbook Action Steps

You can network in all kinds of ways, many of which relate to the other chapters in this book. For example, you could find a society that embodies your brand and attend their conferences. You could go back to your list of identified thought leaders within your space and get to know them. Find ways to not only start networking, but to dive deeper in those relationships.

Here are a few practical ways to get your networking going today.

1. Go back to your spreadsheet list of thought leaders (from Chapter 4). Include a "goal" column in your spreadsheet. What is your goal if you meet those thought leaders? You might write "mentor, partner, event organizer, part of my ecosystem, funding."

2. Go to your conferences tab on the spreadsheet. Identify and mark the conferences you can attend in the next two months. Make a column to list who is going to be there that you want to meet. If you don't have access to the attendee list, that's fine. You almost always have access to the names of the speakers, organizers, or sponsors attending. Add any additional local events that are directly relevant to your goal and business model that could be good for networking.

3. Commit to attend two of the identified events in the next two months, with the goal of meeting or deepening relationships. If you have the time available, feel free to commit to four to eight events in the next two months. Put them on your calendar as soon as you identify them.

    a. Beginner networker or introvert: get to know at least two people per event.

    b. Advanced networker or extrovert: get to know at least six people per event.

    c. Remember to add them to LinkedIn after you meet them!

4. Create a database of networking contacts.

    a. a. Find all the business cards lying around the office and home and put them in an envelope.

    b. Get a virtual assistant or hire someone to scan everything into a spreadsheet. If you were going to do it yourself, you probably would have done so by now. So outsource it today so it is off your list. I've used virtual assistants, TaskRabbit, and paid interns for this task. Choose the platform (TaskRabbit, Leverage, Upwork) and post a job, ranging from $10 to $40 an hour—$10 for a paid intern, $40 for on-demand virtual assistants.

    c. Upload the spreadsheet of cards to LinkedIn in order to automatically connect with everyone.

    d. Going forward, every time you come home from a conference, go through every business card and connect on LinkedIn.

Chapter 8

· · · · · · · • ⬤   ⬤ • · · · · · · ·

Preparing for Your First Presentation

Many people are scared of public speaking. In fact, public speaking is frequently listed as a top fear, more feared than death.

For the thought leader, keynote presentations are an important tool and can be both impactful and extremely lucrative. They have become one of my top revenue streams. To ensure you are ready to handle the fear related to speaking, the next two chapters will go into detail on how to prepare everything you need for successful speaking gigs, and then how to actually get on stage.

Elements of a Great Keynote

First things first: you need to create an actual presentation keynote, which includes everything from the storyline to the slides. There are a lot of companies and consultants that can help you build that first presentation. I made sure to invest money and time into this part of my thought leader foundation. It was helpful to have professionals working with me on the personal story part of the keynote because I was trying to condense my struggle with a thirteen-year misdiagnosis, forty-three hospitalizations, and six major surgeries into ninety seconds of compelling content. It's really easy to include too many details. Professional script writers and designers can help create that perfect package that takes the audience on an emotional journey without them feeling emotions you don't want them to feel, like pity or boredom.

When you are preparing for a keynote, you want to think through the primary elements that create a great presentation. By making sure your talk has each of the following elements, you will be set up for success.

Passion

If you asked me to share what I believe has propelled my career forward more than anything, I would say infectious passion. All great salespeople and leaders possess this. Their excitement and energy are so strong and authentic that others can't help but smile and want to be a part of what they're doing. All great actors and musicians have it as well. They have the ability to make you feel along with them, take you on an emotional journey, and even change your mood. The strength of their belief washes over you, and makes you believe too.

Passion is key when it comes to keynotes. When you speak, you are both a salesperson and teacher. You are selling ideas, not products or services, and you are communicating those ideas in new ways so that your listeners will remember them. It is a performance; the packaging of the content into stories and the actual physical delivery are the two most important parts of a keynote.

Credibility and Storytelling

This element includes why you are an expert, and why the audience should trust you and your content.

Your goal is always to connect with the audience. Listing a bunch of credentials such as job title, educational background, or past accomplishments is not interesting or compelling. Reading from a bio is not interesting or compelling either. For information anyone can read on LinkedIn, let them read it there. On stage, the best way to establish credibility in a way that connects to the audience is through storytelling. This is one of the most important skills you can develop as a thought leader. If you package your *why* into a narrative arc for the listener, you can weave other aspects of your credibility into that story and show the audience your passion.

> ## Don't tell people you're passionate. Show them.

Claremont Graduate University Center for Neuroeconomics Studies found a fascinating scientific link between storytelling and empathy. During an experiment, researchers drew blood samples from participants, then showed the subjects a video of a person telling a story. Finally, they obtained a second round of blood samples. The Claremont researchers discovered that the second group of blood samples had more oxytocin than the first. Oxytocin is the hormone the brain releases when someone feels a bond with someone else.

The human brain also looks for patterns, and a story is the ultimate pattern. It has a beginning, a middle, and an end. There is usually a moral and a logical ebb and flow. They stir empathy in your audience, and they make you seem wiser and more trustworthy.

My first foray into storytelling was at the age of nine, taking magic lessons. All great magicians know that storytelling is part of the magic behind their illusions. They draw you in with a promise, take you through a range of emotions, and then surprise you at the end, bringing the story to a satisfying conclusion. You want to learn to do the same in your storytelling.

You can study storytelling every day by just looking for it. Learn how others tell stories by analyzing your favorite fiction or your favorite movies. Growing up, I read an enormous amount of sci-fi. These types of books are so engrossing because the stories are told so well. They paint a picture of a whole other world and characters' lives. When I read them, it was like watching a movie in my head. Consider a story you might want to share in your presentation. What would the storyline look like if it was a movie? The more you can visualize it, the better.

Use your personal experiences so that the audience connects you to your ideas. The overriding theme of my story is perseverance and success in the face of adversity. I might share about my physician mom dying of cancer, my struggle with a thirteen-year

181

misdiagnosis, or the sexual harassment and gender bias I've faced. I don't use any of these hardships as a crutch, but instead as a catalyst and opportunity to make a major difference. There is an opportunity side to everything; you just have to see it. It's usually right there in front of you. I now both invest and work on oncology startups to treat or cure cancer. My ultimate diagnosis of Crohn's disease is what drove me to set a life goal of impacting one hundred million patients or more. The gender bias led to my turning myself into a professional speaker and launching this new platform to help others become known for their brains. I took these three hardships and traumas in my past and used them as an opportunity and catalyst to do massive good. Always engage listeners emotionally so they understand what the ideas you're sharing mean to you. As we covered at the very beginning of the book, you want to know and share why you do what you do.

Think about the main theme of your story. Do you have a trauma, hardship, or unfair situation you can turn around and turn into an opportunity? Remember, whenever one door closes, always other doors open up, and paths appear. You just have to have the courage to step through the door and down that new path. That is your personal story.

What will capture people's attention and emotions? You want the audience to be able to root for you. Know your story arc. Know your two or three main points that you want the audience to understand and have a clear conclusion or the summary. You can get creative with the conclusion. Many speakers wait to share the conclusion until the end of their talk, which keeps listeners on the edge of their seat.

You don't necessarily have to tell a personal story. You could tell a story of someone else, as long as it connects to the audience emotionally. As you tell this story, be sure to include the setup, the confrontation, and the resolution. Maybe your hero set off on a grand adventure to climb the world's highest peak (the setup). Then illustrate the troubles this person faces along the way. Perhaps they get stuck somewhere (the confrontation). Build the suspense, and then show how the problem was resolved (the resolution). This is an extremely common formula for storytelling and works to both engage listeners emotionally and inspire them.

The best and most compelling stories are about overcoming hardship, persevering, epiphanies leading to behavior change, or going through something traumatic and turning that trauma into something better. The common theme to all of these situations is inspiration. What have you done, seen, experienced, know about, caused, reacted to, or changed that can serve as inspiration for others? Whether on stage or in person, people may not remember what you say, but they will almost always remember how you made them feel.

Using Storytelling Formulas

Earlier in the book, we talked about Simon Sinek's Golden Circle Formula. The key to his formula is to focus on the reason you're doing what you're doing. You can use this formula to prepare your presentation as well. Start by explaining why you chose your occupation, what personal aspirations fueled your professional desires, and why you are working on the project you are now working on. Once your incentives are clear, describe how your brand is fulfilling those motives. Finally, talk through what your specific solutions are.

Along with credibility and storytelling, think about how to build audience engagement into your presentation. I once gave a presentation at a New York City nightclub for a biotech company. They had rented it out to have an evening event with speakers and a panel. The place was crowded, and people were drinking, so they were happy, chatty, and loud. When I started sharing my story, I suddenly had two-hundred people staring at me. It was completely quiet in the nightclub, because I had grabbed their attention. I used this to my advantage and asked a question. I said, "Have you ever just woken up out of bed and been ready to go?" The whole audience lifted up, and they nodded. They were on the emotional ride with me. The more you can connect in a personal way like this, the more they will be engaged. Questions can help to build that connection.

Elon Musk frequently uses a particular storytelling formula in his keynotes. He describes a problem consumers currently face, connects it to listeners, and then paints a picture of what the world would be like if the problem no longer existed. This technique can awaken the listeners' optimism. Next, Elon discusses the challenges that stand in the way of a solution, which convinces people he's not a hopeless idealist. Rather, he demonstrates that he's considered every aspect of the issue. He uses data to explain how his team has found a way to resolve that dilemma. In short, the formula lets you put yourself in the audience's shoes and anticipate their responses. This story formula includes: a problem, a view of a nonproblem world, challenges to eradicating that problem, and data to resolve that problem.

Nancy Duarte is a famous author and speaker. She's also an expert on storytelling and engaging an audience in a corporate presentation. She has a simple, but powerful formula. If you Google her name, you can watch her TED talk about it. In short, the formula consists of two parts: what is and what could be. Essentially, the speaker toggles back and forth between those two categories. This formula keeps an audience engaged when reviewing a product or service, but you could also use it to share an idea. Describe the hardship of not having the benefit that comes from the idea, and then describe the convenience the idea does provide. Don't get straight to the solution. As humans, we are often most engaged when we feel the problem or pain first.

Don't Be the Drone-On Guy

Not to be confused with cool, autonomous-flying drones, the drone-on guy is that uncool speaker, friend or coworker who takes way too long to tell a story. If you've ever interacted with eight-year-olds, you know exactly what I mean. No story, no matter how shocking, surprising, or potentially impactful is interesting if you drone on with too many facts or details. One of the biggest errors I see people make is spending too much time on your personal story.

Yes, you definitely need the personal story, but most of the details can be deleted. Get it down to the back of the napkin. Delete all repetitive words, ideas, and harping. In fact, delete every single word that doesn't directly prove your main point. Tangents and irrelevant, repetitive, or unnecessary details are the main killers of good stories.

Keynote Endings

The key to concluding is to leave your audience in a way that they will remember you and what you shared.

Be careful of giving too many takeaways. My rule of thumb is that presentations under twenty minutes should have no more than three takeaways. When I do fifteen-minute keynotes, I typically get two points across: patients are empowered by technology, and healthcare is moving out of the clinic and into the home. By focusing in this way, I can really drive those points home throughout the talk and again in the conclusion.

To end on a high note, you could close with a vivid overview of what life is like with your takeaways. If you use this method, you should strive to paint an enticing picture, one that's full of colorful phrases.

Finally, consider inspiring your audience with a clear call to action at the end of your presentation. Without a call to action, the audience might say, "Okay, that was fun, and I learned a few things, but I don't know how to implement what I learned." Give them those action items to put your ideas into practice.

Creating a Slide Deck

The gold standard for presentations is Microsoft's PowerPoint. I like to design and edit my slides in Apple's Keynote software and then save it as PowerPoint. If I get the main slide deck created by a designer, I have them do it in PowerPoint. That is the software the majority of AV technicians are used to working with and have loaded on the computers. Though a lot of us in Silicon Valley use Macs, which means you might be used to designing in Keynote, the event space and AV techs almost always use PCs with Microsoft software.

As an event planner, I know how important a speaker's choice of slide deck software can be for a smooth, uninterrupted presentation. At a major event, you need everything to run smoothly, and there are a lot of moving pieces. If a speaker were to come with a different format than PowerPoint, that could cause delays. In the worst-case scenario, the computer might even crash while you are on stage. That happened to me at one of my earliest keynotes. I was on stage, and the computer crashed multiple times, likely because of software incompatibility. Not only was it distracting for both myself and the audience, but it interrupted the storyline I was presenting.

I've seen speakers and AV teams work for an hour or more right before an event begins, frantically trying to get a presentation stable and running because the software wasn't compatible. This is stressful for the event team, and especially stressful for you. Do you want the hour leading up to your keynote to consist of fighting with a computer, anxiously trying to get it to work in time? The point is that using anything other than PowerPoint is risky, unless the speaker instructions specifically list other formats for your slides.

Secondly, I make sure to use a completely static deck. Nothing animated, no sound, no videos at all. Those three elements are much more likely to make an AV system crash. If there's an issue with your slides, you and the audience will be distracted. In my past experience running events, rarely does a deck containing sound, video, or animations work correctly. The vast majority of the time, even with an expensive professional AV team, videos are problematic. They are always an added stress for the AV team, and will take more of your time just to send over to the team than a simple, static deck. Why waste your valuable time discussing back and forth formats and ways for the AV team to handle your video? In addition, why would you take an audience's attention away from your storyline by breaking it up with a video? They can see your videos online. And I haven't even mentioned that the lighting might be also be terrible to be able to clearly see a video.

With sound, including video sound, you are relying on a lot of hardware that might be bad quality, not loud enough, full of static. Connectors from the computer to the speakers might be missing or incompatible. There are so many things that can go wrong when having to play sound while on stage. Just don't do it. It's very high risk for something that is actually a distraction and not value-add most of the time. YOU are the storyteller. To be the most professional you can be, forget about doing anything fancy with your slides. Your slides should just be illustrating your point simply, not making your point for you. Include a basic fade between them, and otherwise make them simple and static.

Of course, all of this is assuming you have a slide deck, and you should, especially if you're a new speaker or are just building a new platform. Why? It provides structure. When speakers don't have structure, that leaves room for errors. Some people, like John Hagel, excel in speaking without structure. This is called narrative speaking. But most speakers benefit from having a reference point, especially when they are getting started. I now have over one hundred different slide decks, and I've personalized every single one to the audience and event. As with content, once you have one foundational slide deck created, others become much easier to put together. Below are a few of the specific benefits of having a slide deck:

- They serve as a reminder or a trigger for you to present specific content, especially facts and figures. They will help you stay on track with your message and not accidentally go off into a tangent.

- They give the audience a photo, an illustration, graph, or key point that can help drive a message home and help them stay with the overall story line.

- The audience can take photos of the slides to remember key points or to share on social media.

THE THOUGHT LEADER FORMULA

Unless you are a designer or have a lot of experience working with slide design, hire a designer for your slides! Again, focus on your strengths. Obviously, you need to craft what content will go on each slide, but you shouldn't be sitting around figuring out if there should be a triangle here or a line there. More importantly, a professionally designed deck makes you appear professional.

Choose a specific color scheme that relates to your brand. For example, the original high-end designer I used for my first deck came up with a color scheme of a black background as a differentiator, with blue as the main font color. Keep in mind, you will use the template of colors you create for years.

If you build your story line and deck in almost self-contained sections of five to ten minutes per section, it makes it extremely easy to quickly build a deck of any length of time. The more flexible you are with presentation length, the easier it is for organizers to work with you and fit you into their conference agenda. That means you have many more opportunities than you might otherwise have with a rigid length.

My healthcare-focused keynotes range from six minutes to 120 minutes. The way I am able to be so flexible is that my two-hour long presentation is built using this section technique. I know how long each section is, so if an event asks me for a thirty-eight-minute keynote, I can easily put a deck together by just pasting together certain sections. The twelve healthcare sections can be reduced in size by deleting a few slides to fit the time limit exactly or increased by just adding a few examples.

Here is an example of how I break down a two-hour healthcare presentation:

- Intro and credibility, including my *why*: two to five minutes

- Explanation of exponential vs. linear: ten to twelve minutes

- Healthcare delivery shift: telemedicine and point of care diagnostics: ten to fifteen minutes

- Drones: five to seven minutes

- Genomics and microbiome: five to ten minutes

- Cloud storage and computing: four to ten minutes

- Artificial intelligence: seven to twenty minutes

- Sensors: six to fifteen minutes

- Virtual reality: three to ten minutes

- 3D printing: five to ten minutes

- Health coaching: two to seven minutes

- Self-care: five to fifteen minutes

- Conclusion: two to ten minutes

Practice, Practice, Practice

Once you have the slides and story line perfected, now it's time to practice. This doesn't mean running through your deck a couple times. This means putting in hardcore time and effort until you can recite your keynote in your sleep. If you're not willing to put in the work rehearsing and refining, you won't come across as a professional thought leader or experienced speaker. The less experienced you seem on stage, with "ums" or "ahs" or delays, the harder it will be to get booked for other engagements. Your goal is to say "um" zero times on stage.

You need to know your content inside and out. Once you know your content down cold, you can go on autopilot on stage when it comes to the words and focus on connecting with the audience, how you're moving, and your delivery speed.

Everybody gets nervous and has some degree of stage fright for their first talk. The easiest way to become completely paralyzed, though, is by forgetting your words. This is why you want to be overly prepared.

Steve Jobs famously spent months preparing for his keynotes and practiced them more relentlessly than even I do. For every minute he was on stage, he spent hours rehearsing. Behind the scenes, he was intensely involved with every stage and aspect of creating his keynote. His presentations helped propel Apple to the marketing powerhouse that it became. His formula for success boiled down to three things: storytelling, emotional connection, and effective preparation. Jobs' passion for what he was talking about came through in every movement and every word. People who seem to speak effortlessly, as he did, only do so because they spend a massive amount of effort beforehand preparing.

Preparation equals confidence. The more prepared you are, the more confident you'll be. Even without looking at your slides, you'll walk on stage confident.

The first ten to fifteen rehearsals, you're going to see where you want to change around a slide or change up some phrasing. You're going to forget your facts and figures and have to look them up. The next five to ten rehearsals are when you will have the presentation perfectly worded and arranged. You should be able to do it at least three times in a row without pausing or making any mistakes. The first perfect run through doesn't mean you are ready, though. That perfect run through needs to be repeatable, at least twice more, if not three to four or five times more. Then you're ready.

For my first keynote, which was twenty-five minutes long, I practiced forty times. I hired a speaker coach who recorded me and showed me small things I could tweak, such as phrasing or how I held my arms. I then watched that video every day for over a month or played it in the background while I was doing other tasks.

To this day, I practice every keynote at least twice, if not five to ten times before I give it. I recently gave a sixty-minute keynote with some new material, in front of an audience of 2,700 medical office groups. This was also a full-pay keynote through my speaker bureau, so I was extra cognizant of wanting to give a flawless performance. I practiced that particular keynote ten times, even with my extensive stage experience. That came out to ten hours of practice.

It takes a lot of hard work and time to look effortless on stage. That's the interesting thing about practice. Some people say, "Oh, I don't want to appear over practiced and scripted." In fact, it's those speakers who don't practice enough that come out wooden, as if they were reading from a script, because they haven't fully mastered the keynote. Once you master it perfectly, it will sound effortless, conversational, and natural on stage.

Of course, there is some resistance that comes with practicing the same content repeatedly. Anyone who needs to practice something over and over, whether for competing or performing, understands this. Everyone wants to skip a day or a week. It's easy to justify by saying, "You know what? I'm good enough, and I can stop there." However, what separates achievers from the super-achievers is that super-achievers go the extra mile, even when it's difficult, boring, repetitive, or exhausting. They see that bigger picture and understand it's the repetitive hard work that will propel them to success.

For that first keynote I mentioned above, I was getting tired of doing it over and over by the twentieth run-through. By the thirtieth time through, I started to dread it, in my head saying, "Nooo, not again!" It was torture! But then by run-through thirty-five, I realized the delivery and story line were perfect, and I was so incredibly happy I made the effort. I only had five run-throughs to go to achieve my goal, and I was able to practice the last couple on the actual stage I would be using. To this day, I am still grateful I made that much of an effort.

Tips and Tricks

Fortunately, there are a few tips and tricks you can use when still learning your content. First, you can hire someone to transcribe one of your video talks. That way, when you go to give new talks, you have your content in a whole other form to ingrain it into your brain—an actual script.

When I did this, my script had every single fact and figure I say on the stage. I could look back on it and read it over and over. Sometimes on plane rides to the speaking engagement, I would read that transcript, which solidified it in my head.

Another trick is to listen to a video of your talk one to two times a day. Have it playing in the background while you are getting dressed in the morning or typing up emails. If you have your keynote constantly running in the background, the phrases and ideas will become firmly lodged in your memory.

Having your content memorized is helpful for Q&A as well. Challenge yourself with questions people might ask and prepare your answers to them. Experts appear as experts on stage during Q&A because they prepare or have spent years saying the same phrasing over and over again. Their answers come immediately and eloquently.

After you come up with questions for yourself, give your keynote to someone else and ask them to quiz you on it. What questions do they have after they hear your talk? Be sure to be able to answer those questions thoroughly. Being a guest on podcasts is another great way to hone your Q&A practice in a less stressful environment than a live, in-person audience. If you have prepared answers, the phrasing will come out smoothly. You will get to a point where you just automatically have fantastic phrasing for almost any question people will throw at you, even under pressure.

Invest in Your Voice

There are many different ways you can invest in your voice so that you can improve your presentations. Don't skip over this section, thinking if you prepare enough, you'll be fine. Without outside feedback, you will be good, but not great. Invest the time and money to be great. This is an essential investment into *You, Inc.*

Voice Coaches

A big question for most newbie speakers is whether or not they need a voice coach. The best speakers enunciate every word clearly and use voice inflection to drive points home. If you could use practice in either of those areas, I recommend investing in a voice coach.

If you have a heavy American regional accent, if English is a second language and you have a heavy accent, or if you are a rapid talker and your words merge into one another (as mine sometimes do), a voice coach can help you pronounce words and sentences in a way that are more universally understood, both in the US and internationally. Many of your speaking engagements may have a number of non-native English speakers in the audience. You might potentially have an accent that they're not used to hearing, which means they're not going to understand a significant amount of what you're saying.

I'm personally a huge fan of accents—domestic, regional, and foreign accents. I love listening to them. In fact, a lot of people find them charming and interesting. When you speak on stage, however, no one can ask you to clarify if they miss something, or to repeat a sentence they didn't understand. I once watched an interesting presentation by a highly experienced speaker. Though the content was amazing, I missed many of the words and concepts because I spent most of the time translating his accent in my head, to understand what words he was actually saying. By the time I had figured one sentence out, I had already missed his next two sentences. You have to be able to speak clearly and concisely. You can, of course, revert to your normal, full accent offstage, but on stage you need to adjust so the entire audience understands your main message.

If you are a native-born English speaker, you might have read that paragraph and thought, "This doesn't apply to me." However, consider the fact that many actors and actresses hire voice coaches. They understand that their voice is a major tool in their career. Voice coaches can help you get your message across in the best way. They can help you enunciate, slow down or speed up, keep your voice up, lighten your voice, focus on inflection and pauses, and more. One frequent mistake people make is to end a sentence on a high note, as if it were a question. A voice coach can help retrain your speech to end your sentence on a deeper note.

My stage voice is different from my socializing voice. On stage, I lower my voice, speak more slowly and make sure to enunciate every word, because it comes across more powerfully than my higher-pitched social voice. You have to remember that it's not just what you say, but the way you say it. Get them with attitude.

Speaker Coaches

Do you need a speaker coach? Yes. While the voice coach works on your voice and you may or may not need that, a speaker coach is going to look at the whole presentation and help you work on body movement, stance, and your overall story line arc. They help you go from "90 percent there" to the next level.

You can benefit by having even one session with a good speaker coach. I had two sessions with two different coaches. In total, it only took two or three hours of my time. Cost for hiring speaker coaches ranges from a couple of hundred dollars to a couple of thousand dollars an hour. I hired high-end coaches, because I know you often get what you pay for.

To find a good speaker coach, use every resource at your disposal. You can use social media to find a good coach. You can post that you're looking for speaker coach recommendations in your area and ask people to tag or comment on good coaches. Your best bet is to find coaches that are recommended by your network. Both of the ones I used came highly recommended by speaker friends.

When you see a speaker coach, make sure you have your presentation finished and prepared, so you can practice. You should view them as people who help you put the icing on the cake. They aren't there to help you brainstorm what you want to say. They'll video record you, analyze different aspects of the overall presentation like phrasing, body language, speed, story lines, facial expression, and eye contact. They'll give you feedback on how the audience might perceive you. I was reminded to slow down my speech and open my arms wide to take up more space because I'm so petite. My coaches also pointed out a couple of sentences I could rephrase for clarity and impact. This kind of feedback is invaluable.

Improv

In addition to hiring voice and speaker coaches, you can also look into taking improv classes. Improv helps you think quickly and get used to being in front of a crowd, even if it's just the other people in the class. It forces you to think about your overall body language, voice, and words as one complete item. I took classes with the "Comedy Magician," Robert Strong, in the Bay

Area. He is a fantastic emcee, moderator, magician, and improv guy.

Improv can also be great for anyone who's in business. It helps you hone many skills, such as communication, reaction, timing, teamwork, and active listening. If you're a beginner speaker, improv classes are great ways to get comfortable in your own skin and see how others react to you.

Acting Coach or Consultant

While acting coaches are usually for actors playing a role, they can help you, too. Great stage actors portray emotion in their voice, use silent pauses, and leverage body language to tell the story. If you're not normally an expressive person, an acting lesson or two can go a long way. Whereas improv teaches you to think on your feet, acting lessons can teach you to tell a story without using words. You're not trying to be an actor, but you do need to prepare your own version of a one-person play. You can take acting classes with a group or simply hire an acting coach for a few sessions.

Speaking on stage is a performance.

You can also hire a consultant for private lessons or small group classes. If you want to learn from someone in particular and they're not officially a consultant, you can still suggest it to them. See if they'd be willing to share their advice with you for an hour for a certain price. The cost for a consultant can range anywhere from $100 an hour to $2,000 an hour or more. If you're asking someone who doesn't normally consult on the side, you can suggest an amount and make it easy on them by working with their schedule.

You can find a consultant through platforms like Upwork or through social media connections. Have them come to your office or home. If they teach a class and you have the time, take the class so you can learn from your classmates. You get to practice speaking and moving in front of a safe group in a safe environment, which will ultimately help you once you're on stage. In a class, you can safely screw up and do whatever feels right for you.

Workbook Action Steps

We've covered a lot in this chapter. Now it's time to put some of your learning into practice.

Here are a few points to remember when preparing to speak:

1. What key points will establish your credibility? Pick one or two storytelling formulas that would shape your content. This is your *why* packaged up in a one- to three-minute introduction.

2. What audience engagement questions seem to flow from your narrative arc and content? How can you get the audience emotionally engaged and responding?

3. What three points do you want your audience to take away?

4. Hire a presentation or script writer to help you create that first story line. (optional)

5. Spend ten minutes searching Upwork, TaskRabbit, or ask your friends for recommendations for a PowerPoint slide designer, if you don't bring on a script writer company that designs the slides.

6. Create a checklist for practicing your keynote. Write down how many times you practice it.

7. Choose which coaches and classes you want to pursue to improve your stage presence and presentation delivery. Options include: voice coach, speaker coach, improv classes, acting classes. Find options through friends or by a Google or LinkedIn search.

Chapter 9

· · · · · · · ● · · · ● · · · · · · · · ·

On Stage

Now that you've prepared for your first presentation, the next step is to become an active speaker–on stage. You can speak monthly, or even weekly–whatever fits with your overall goals and plan. The point is, you can build yourself to a point where you have so many requests to be on stage. You can choose which conferences you say yes to, and you might get to a point where you even need to turn a large number of requests down.

First consider how many events you'd like to speak at within the next two years. You can start the clock immediately after you have all your material in order. Set the goal after you're ready. My goal was fifty speaking arrangements within four years. By being intentional with my time, goals, and money, I ended up surpassing my own goal by years, greatly exceeding my own high expectations. That's an underlying theme I apply to every area of my life—to always exceed expectations, even my own, by a considerable amount.

It's rare for someone to have experience in business development, events, and professional speaking. Because I have done all three, I have a unique perspective when it comes to getting on stage. I can show you the behind the scenes so that you can exceed your own expectations.

> **It's time to get behind the scenes!**

Types of Events and What They Pay

One thing to note is that event nomenclature is not standardized, and while one group might call something a seminar, others might call that a workshop, meeting, conference, symposium, forum, summit, congress, or convention. Don't give too much weight to what the organizers are calling the event.

As you'll learn in this chapter, there are many factors besides the event name to consider when analyzing where to spend your efforts.

The questions I repeatedly hear from aspiring speakers are about what they should charge, what types of events will pay speaker fees (also called honorariums), and which events will at least cover their travel and hotel expenses. The reality is the answers are all over the board. For some events, you'll speak entirely for free; you might even have to pay for your ticket and travel expenses. Some will cover the cost of your travel and accommodations, and others might pay large fees of $5,000 to $50,000 or more. Some will even cover the costs of a five-star experience, with business class flights and a week at a five-star resort.

Corporations, nonprofits, public-facing conferences, universities, university associations, academic conferences, and private conferences all offer opportunities to speak. It's about understanding what events can afford and which ones are worth your time.

Keep in mind that some of the events that require you to pay for your own hotel, flights, and even a conference ticket might be a good use of your time and money. Giant conferences like SXSW and DEFCON require you to pay for your own ticket if you are chosen as a panelist (versus an invited speaker), but if you were planning on attending anyway, being on a panel is just a huge bonus.

While keynotes can be a great revenue stream, you likely have goals beyond being a full-time speaker. The point is to understand your business model and goals that you outlined in Chapter 1. That will help you decide whether an event is worth your time. In fact, you might be in a place in your career that even if you were offered $25,000 to speak at an event, you would turn it down. Why would you turn down a $25,000 speaking engagement? Imagine you are at a pivotal place in your main business model and revenue stream, and this $25,000 gig would take you away from the office for seven days, something you couldn't possibly do because your other revenue stream has priority. This is why you have to be crystal clear on your overarching goals.

On the flip side, there can be significantly more ROI from keynoting an event than just monetary ROI. Some events may put you in front of the right audience to drive your overall goals. That equals new potential customers, revenue streams, partnerships, investors, and more. Maybe the event produces great videos, with a wide online distribution that could reach your target market. Sometimes you might just want the credibility that comes with speaking at a specific event.

If you love to travel and have always wanted to go to a certain country or city, that alone could be enough ROI for you to speak for free, especially if the event covers the travel and accommodation. Because of the large amount of travel I've done over the past few years for keynotes, I no longer travel for vacation. Instead, I say yes to certain speaking opportunities because I know the experience will be amazing, and worth my time. Sometimes the experience can include VIP parties, special tours not available to the public, and even access to venues or buildings that are off limits for almost everyone, but open for the VIP speakers. The best part, especially with international travel, is you get to be submerged into a culture, and spend quality time with the locals, including politicians and business leaders—something you can't do when you're just on vacation.

Here is a chart you can use as a general reference on who pays for what:

What	Speaker Honorarium/ Fee	Travel & Hotel
Corporations	Usually	Usually
Associations	Usually	Usually
Public-Facing Conferences	Sometimes to Rarely	Usually
Universities/ Colleges	Variable	Variable
Trade Shows (i.e., SXSW, CES)	Rarely to Never	Rarely to Never
Nonprofits	Rarely	Sometimes
Academic Conferences	Rarely to Never	Rarely to Never
TED or TEDx	Never	Sometimes
Unconferences	Never	Never
Meetups	Never	Never
Private Conferences	Completely Variable	Completely Variable

One thing to note: this table does not apply to the most well-known thought leaders or speakers when being asked to speak. Even if none of the other speakers are being paid, or even having their travel covered, sometimes a "big name" is the exception. Some events will raise sponsorship money just to pay for a famous speaker, while everyone else still has to cover their own expenses.

Let's break it down.

Corporations will typically pay up to your full fee plus expenses. With events, it's crucial you understand the event's goals, and you should tailor your content to help the event achieve those goals. Corporations typically run events for four reasons:

1. Education for their employees and consultants

2. Education for their customers, partners, or clients

3. Business development reasons—the audience will consist of potential and current clients

4. Marketing—the event supports branding. This is typically in the form of sponsorships for other events, but can be company led as well

When you look at the first three reasons, it is clear how paying for top speakers translates directly to ROI for the corporation. Corporations also have the budget and ROI to afford to pay speakers. You are essentially a temporary consultant for a clear business reason. Corporations typically choose speakers by committee, through speaker bureaus, by word of mouth, or through personal connections. They will likely also do some research on potential appropriate speakers and find thought leaders in their field, much like you would when searching online for other thought leaders to connect with.

Large affiliations, organizations, and associations for professionals will also pay up to full fee for their main plenary keynote speakers at their main events, which might only have one or two speakers per day. "Plenary" is a term to describe the sessions the entire conference attends. "Simultaneous" sessions happen on multiple stages at one time and divide the attendees. It is much less common to be paid as a panelist for simultaneous sessions.

The reason these large associations can afford to pay for top speakers is because they charge their members an annual membership fee and charge for the event ticket. Combined with money they get from sponsors, they have enough to cover the cost of top speakers. The way they find their main speakers is the same way corporations find speakers. In addition, these large events include a place on their website where people can apply to speak. In general, if you get a speaking engagement by applying to speak, the event likely won't pay you or cover your costs.

Major conventions that have thousands of attendees and giant conglomerates like SXSW and CES (which had 182,000 attendees in 2018) don't typically pay for speakers, and don't cover travel or hotel. The exception can be that major celebrity name, but otherwise, some of these events will even charge you full admission if you're a speaker. The ROI for you will come from other ways, and some of these events can be worth the investment.

Academic conferences typically charge the speakers the admission ticket price, and don't cover the hotel or travel. If you have a subject that can fit into an academic conference agenda, this is one of the easiest stages to get on to practice. Just go to the academic conference website and apply. As long as you are relevant, you should get a place on at least a simultaneous session small stage.

Universities and colleges can be variable, but if you're asked to give one or two presentations as a guest, don't expect a large fee. If you sign on as reoccurring faculty, like any other "job," the amount you'll be paid is negotiable. Student organizations or associations within universities or colleges could potentially afford to pay a speaker fee, depending on how well funded the organization is. These entities find speakers the same way corporations do and can additionally have speakers apply to speak.

Public-facing conferences—those that allow the public to buy a ticket—usually can't afford to pay for speakers. If the event is hundreds of dollars to attend, they likely don't have the budget to pay speaker fees, unless they have a large amount of sponsorship. Don't expect to be paid a fee for conferences accessible to the public and ticket prices under $1,000 or even $2,000. Once they get more expensive than that, and if the event has large corporate sponsors, they might be able to afford to pay some speakers. The costs of running events is so variable, partially dependent on the venue and food costs, which are two large budget line items. In my experience, most public-facing events will try to get all their speakers for free, as the less they pay the speakers, the more profit they'll make. Some will want you to cover your own expenses. You know, simple math. An event is a business and needs to make money.

Nonprofits are variable. If you're dealing with a small nonprofit, or one without a lot of funding, they can't afford to pay speaker fees. If it's a large nonprofit with strong revenue streams, then they could potentially afford a speaker fee. If they have a small budget, then they may still be able to cover your travel and accommodations. It doesn't hurt to ask. The key here is to find out the goals for the event to understand if they would be willing to cover costs or give a speaker fee.

TEDx events are both nonprofit and public facing. Don't expect to be paid a speaker fee for TEDx. The ticket prices are low, and the sponsorship funding relatively scarce. A speaker is lucky if the individual TEDx event can scrape together enough funding to cover travel and accommodations. Your ROI with a TEDx is the recorded video, and the potential for that video to get a lot of views. The way you get on stage at a TEDx is to apply online, or simply know someone on the event team. There are so many TEDx events; you could have someone on your team identify relevant themed ones and apply to them for you. You can see all the TEDx events on the main TED website. In 2017, there were over 5,000 worldwide.

Unconferences and meetups don't pay speaker fees, and don't cover travel and hotel. Unconferences are participant driven. Most, if not all, of the participants can give a presentation or run a workshop during simultaneous sessions. They typically have very small budgets, and there is often no cost to attend. You only have to be invited and cover your own travel and accommodation. This is true for attendees and speakers. Meetups are small, local events, typically just two to three hours long, with little to no funding. It's easy to get on stage at both unconferences and meetups. Once you or your team has identified the relevant ones, contact the organizer for an invitation. With meetups, just contact the organizer listed on the website, and offer to speak.

Nontraditional Events You Can Use to Practice Your New Skill

Keep in mind that speaking engagements can take on many forms. Your goal when you first begin speaking is just get that practice in front of people. Once you are fully confident with your new keynote—the slides are done, you have practiced enough alone, hired a coach if needed—now getting that practice in front of a live audience is crucial.

For those very first live audiences, you can get creative. You can do a one-time event at your home. You could host a dinner party with five friends and give the keynote during dessert. Invite a few other friends over, so each of you can give fifteen-minute keynotes.

Or host an actual unconference for a day and have attendees sign up to give short presentations.

Think about that safe zone for you to practice and develop your skills of being in front of a live audience. If your home or office isn't a good venue, you can rent an on-demand office or event space for a few hundred dollars through platforms like Breather or LiquidSpace. Because these platforms are constantly changing, do a search for "the Airbnb for office space and events" in your area. It's worth investing in yourself to get some practice in low-stress environments.

You can also do those first, early speaking engagements at meetups at the local libraries. You can find opportunities at society annual conferences. If you are a salaried worker, start with a presentation to your department. A great stepping stone to keynotes is to be on a panel. Participate in something like Renaissance Weekend, an event held multiple times a year in different parts of the US, where everyone who attends is required to be on a panel.

Local town hall events, community centers, small local association lunches, and local clubs are all potential opportunities. The best way to get on those stages is to attend one of their events and meet the people in charge of them. Offer to speak after you've built the relationship, focusing on how the organization and audience would benefit from your content. Lead with value by focusing on their needs.

Even if you want to get to large events at some point, don't discount the value of smaller events at all stages of your speaker journey. Smaller events are more intimate, making it easier to form deeper connections with the audience. These also provide you with an opportunity to record yourself. With the cameras on our phones, high-resolution video is easily accessible. You could set your phone up on a tripod and have a friend press record.

When you are ready to go bigger, start applying to larger conferences. Go back to the identified conferences tab of your spreadsheet, and just go down the list and apply, and keep track of those you apply to in the spreadsheet. This is also a great task for a virtual assistant, your marketing team, business development team, or any of your support staff or temporary consultants on demand.

Things to Consider

Use one of the previous ways listed to start small and connect with an audience. Once you do that, you're on your way to getting on stage consistently. Let's review a few more important aspects of speaking together.

Pricing

After you have experience speaking, it's time to think about pricing. Assuming you want to speak at corporate or association events—those where you can be paid a fee—how do you price yourself?

Pricing ultimately comes back to your credibility. Say you don't have your book published yet, but you do have ten speaking engagements under your belt, and you know you will come across as a paid professional. If that is the case, you can start charging $500 to $2,500 per keynote. Do that for a couple of keynotes, and then go up to $2,500. I increased my price gradually, and then I made big leaps to $7,500, and ultimately $10,000 to $20,000, all in two years. I started charging by my third speaking engagement. Normally, speakers wouldn't start charging that quickly, but an opportunity fell in my lap. A large corporation found one of my articles on LinkedIn on digital health. They saw the value and hired me for $2,500 and covered travel and hotel. From there, I kept increasing my price. I was able to start charging almost immediately because I put the massive hard work into preparation before ever giving my first keynote, and had built a strong, solid foundation. I went through the required steps, just as you are doing now, assuming you are answering and applying the workbook questions to your life.

223

After you gain experience, the easiest way to price yourself is to lay out the amount you are comfortable charging and add 25 percent. If you add that 25 percent and you gasp, you're probably getting close. Remember, if you aren't living outside your comfort zone, then you aren't growing. Take a deep breath and move forward.

That First Video

To be asked to keynote, you need a video. But to get a video, you need to give a keynote. Catch-22. So you have to get creative to get that first video. If you choose to get keynote practice at your home, office, or rented space as mentioned previously, you can have a friend or videographer set up one to three cameras to record you. Smartphone and tablet cameras are now high enough quality that you don't need an expensive video camera.

Use a video editor or user-friendly software like Cambria to edit and layer in an audience track and put that up on YouTube. I stumbled into this video hack after giving a short presentation at an evening event on the opioid epidemic. Even though it was filmed on a stage with a live audience of about sixty people, the videographer's style focused only on two close-up angles of me. With a black background behind me, you couldn't tell if I was on a stage or in a small room. I also didn't have any B-roll of the audience to edit into the video. But at the end of the video, you could hear the audience clapping. After editing my video to include the audience track, I realized that this could be hacked for new speakers. You can get two to three close-up video shots against a dark background curtain or wall and add in an audience clapping track.

Questions to Ask Each Potential Speaking Engagement

To be clear and know what to expect for each speaking engagement, consider the following questions. You can reference the worksheet template in the "Action Steps" at the end of this chapter.

- Number of attendees

- Attendee description

- Stage time (keynote in main auditorium, panel, moderator, break-out session)

- Time needed to block out on your calendar

- Other speakers and topics

- Speaker budget (What is covered? Travel? Hotel?)

- Speaker honorarium or fee

These are all important point to consider. The answers allow you to gain clarity up front. Be clear on the time requirements. Be clear on who is paying you and how. Who makes the plane and hotel reservations? If you pay for your own flight up front, what is the reimbursement process?

On the spreadsheet, also note the venue address. One time, I landed in Germany at midnight and I had to get to the center of town. I could not find the hotel venue address on my phone and had no idea where I was going. Fortunately, a musician, Izzy Flynn, was performing for the same conference and was on my flight. We met while running between connections earlier in London. If I hadn't met Izzy on that layover, I would have been wandering around Munich at midnight by myself, not knowing where to go. Instead, she saved me by helping figure out the airport train and knowing the hotel address. Get your venue address, contact information, and confirmation number in your calendar, but always put it on that spreadsheet, too, so you have access to everything in one place.

When you attend an event as a speaker, you will be asked questions as well, especially about your keynote. They might ask if they can share your slides, video tape you, and broadcast you on their website and social media. They might even ask if they can add your talk to an educational package. I always say yes. Remember, content is free, people pay for packaging. When people hire me to speak, the want the live version. If they want to distribute it after, then I think of it as free marketing. Some people get up in arms about this. They don't like their content being shared if they aren't going to make a profit off of it. Instead, this is a simple way to be a giver that ultimately benefits the speaker in the long run.

Of course, if you work for a corporation and you are speaking under their brand, you will need to check your contracts to ask your boss about distribution requirements. Some companies are strict about their outward-facing message and may tell you no. Other companies are more relaxed. If you're a salaried employee, be sure to get familiar with your company's brand and ask questions before you speak at an event.

Getting on That Stage

In addition to the previous hints on how events choose their speakers, here are some other ways to get on stage. When you have your foundation of your platform in place, and your keynote perfected, it's time to start applying to more speaking opportunities. First hint: See the "apply to speak" button? Click that! Treat the application like an audition. Tailor your proposals to the audience. Grab a relevant pitch and tweak it to fit the event. This is where copy and paste once again comes in handy, especially if you keep all your bio lengths and presentation descriptions in one place, either on the spreadsheet or in a folder.

Leverage Connections

When it comes to getting on stage, connections help, and are sometimes your best option. When you find people who can advise you, they will lift you up with them. Sometimes, they will be willing to recommend you to speak.

Whenever I'm asked to keynote, if possible, I recommend two to five speakers, and I always make sure at least 50 percent of them are women. Those speakers end up recommending me sometimes as well. Find that group of friends who speak about similar or complementary subjects and help each other.

The best thing about conferences is that you can connect with so many different kinds of people, from speakers, to audience members, to those behind the scenes. I highly recommend making friends with conferences organizers. They can help you network, and when you are finally ready to get on stage, you can reach out to them and see what conferences they are working on and if they have any open spots. It is a great way to have an "in" at conferences.

Hire Someone

If you are having a really tough time getting on stage, then you may want to hire someone to help. I have helped many people get on stage, much like an agent would. Sometimes, you need extra help to get your foot in the door.

Back when I was a speaker manager, I used to actively pitch other speakers for events. I found conferences where their message was relevant and had the right audience. Don't be afraid to ask others to help you get your first couple gigs. Be creative; hire a professional speaker or widely known speaker in your industry to introduce you to the right events. You can offer a flat fee or pay per introduction or per speaking gig.

You have to make this worth their while. They spent years growing their business, and this would be a new, unknown revenue stream for them. Worth their while could mean that you pay them thousands of dollars per gig, even if you aren't getting paid for that speaking gig. Essentially, you are asking them to be the Speaker Business Development Department of You, Inc. This is a great example of how you can create new jobs for others in this new world of work.

Speaker Bureaus

Speaker bureaus are great for well-known and established speakers. Bureaus rarely represent speakers who charge less than $10,000. The way they work is on commission. They typically receive 20 percent to 35 percent of the speaker's fee. The great thing about bureaus is that they do find the gigs for you. They lead generate, negotiate, close, and then manage the entire speaking engagement.

Unless you are already well known, a typical speaker bureau won't represent you. Even if you do get signed with a bureau, that's not a guarantee they will ever book you. The speakers who don't need bureaus to lead generate keynotes are the speakers that are represented. When you are just starting out, it's difficult to get represented by one.

If you do get a gig through a speaker bureau, you will need to be prepared to give almost any length keynote—anywhere between fifteen minutes to two hours. You will also need to tailor the content to the audience and come off relatively flawlessly. The bureau will be your contact point for everything related to that gig. There will typically be one or two calls with the bureau and the event organizers to dive into your content. And they will expect the final slide deck, usually PowerPoint, anywhere from six weeks to one week before the event. If the conference offers any type of education credits for professionals, they are the ones who need the deck up to six weeks before, to have time to review, then edit, then review again.

There are exclusive and nonexclusive contracts with bureaus. Some bureaus require you to be exclusive, meaning if you get paid talks from another source, you will still pay them a commission. But they do work harder for exclusive speakers. Nonexclusive contracts mean you can get paid keynotes booked through any source, and only pay the bureau for the ones they lead generate and close.

There are new platforms and bureaus launching all the time. Each one would have to be analyzed individually, and it's important to take time to see what you are getting if you have to pay up-front fees to be listed by them.

Your Checklists for the Stage

Now that we've discussed how to get on a stage, it's time to consider how to actually handle the stage. Once you're there, what do you do? Here, I'll share what I've learned to do through my speaking experience.

Dealing with Stage Fright

Stage fright—we all get it. It happens to 100 percent of people, even sociopaths. Here are some of the best tricks you can use:

- **Do deep breathing exercises right before you get on stage.** Use the Wim Hof Method (WHM) or other deep breathing techniques to oxygenate your muscles and your blood. This way, you don't have to worry about hyperventilating or not being able to breathe enough on stage. There are variations of the WHM, but all are similar. They consist of three stages. Start with controlled hyperventilation for two minutes. Then blow the breath out, and when you need to breathe take a deep breath and hold it. Then when you need to breathe again, take a quick breath while still holding the large breath. Do NOT try to do this for the first time ever right before getting on stage; it can make you light headed. If you practice this for a few days leading up to the event, you can do it on the day of. That way, on stage your muscles are fully oxygenated, so if you get too nervous and start breathing quickly, your body is prepared.

- **Try to walk the stage beforehand.** The night before my talk or at lunch break, I like to get up on stage and walk around on it. I always feel that flutter of stage fright, even though it's an empty room. It lasts only a couple seconds, but then I relax. I like to get that out of the way before the audience enters. The point is to familiarize yourself with the space before the pressure is on. This one trick can make a huge difference.

- **Be authentic with your audience.** For those first speaking events, a nice trick my speaker coach Bronwyn Saglimbeni taught me is to tell the audience it is one of your first talks and that you're nervous. Then the audience will root for you, and you will feel better sharing truthfully. By sharing that first truth, they may forgive a lot more than they would have otherwise.

- **Remind yourself that you know your content.** You acted like Steve Jobs; you rehearsed until you practically fell down. You know your stuff inside and out. Even if you do get nervous, your brain can go on autopilot with the words.

- **Have a good friend in the audience.** Make sure this is someone who you know is rooting for you without judgment and who doesn't make you nervous. When you're on stage, you can look at them and see them as an anchor. This could be your close, nonjudgmental friend, colleague, trusted employee, or even a relative. The key here is to find someone who is nonjudgmental. Sometimes the people closest to us in our lives are going to be the ones that are going to make us the most nervous—like parents, spouses, or children. If that's the case for you, make sure they aren't present for your first talks.

- **Find an anchor in the audience.** Even if you don't know anyone in the audience, always find one or two anchors. Most of the time, these people will be complete strangers. From the very beginning of the talk, they're the ones who are watching you intently. They are incredibly interested in what you are doing, and they are probably nodding along with you. I find those people right away, so I have someone to connect with and keep me centered. I know they're on my side by their head movements and facial expressions.

- **Wear comfortable clothes.** You don't want to be stumbling around. If your straps are showing, if your dress or pant leg rises up, if you have to constantly be fixing something, the audience will notice. I have seen speakers get on stage in shoes they don't know how to walk in, with a hole in their t-shirt, and with a shirt that was too small, showing belly, which I'm sure was not his intention. Fiddling with your outfit makes it look like you're nervous, and the audience won't know it's because of your clothes or shoes. Wear an authentic outfit that fits well so that you don't risk malfunctions.

- **Make sure you wear things that won't show sweat.** Some stages can be incredibly hot. It depends on the stage lights, the venue, the number of people in the venue, weather, and finicky thermostats. Even if the audience is freezing, the stage can be a completely different temperature. Don't wear shirts that show sweat. Light colors are usually the most obvious. I typically wear dark colors because the stage light will only accentuate sweat stains. If you're wondering if the audience can see it, the answer is yes, yes, yes, they can. Wear a suit, jacket, or blazer layer, or wear a dark top, shirt, or dress. White and other light colors can also be seen through on stage, and a stage is NOT the place you want to discover your outfit's transparency rating.

- **Listen to music and dance.** I move and stretch right before I get on stage. This way, I'm not stiff. Instead, I'm happy and relaxed from listening to my favorite music and dancing around.

- **Try to do a full workout and get a full night's sleep the day before every single talk.** That will have a big impact on your psychological state when you are on stage.

- **Don't drink more caffeine than your body is used to.** Doing so will make you shake on stage and have a more rapid heartbeat, which mimics nervousness. I also avoid decongestants for that same reason.

- **Have a small snack beforehand, because your brain needs to have fuel.** Some people like to go on stage without eating anything. In my experience, even four ounces of a protein shake, for example, will make a significant difference in my ability to perform at the level I should be performing at.

- **Use visualization techniques and self-hypnosis.** Imagine the nervousness and stress are flowing out of your body. You can study up on things like self-hypnosis, or get coaches, or a therapist who can help you with visualization techniques.

- **Laugh.** Laughing before you get on stage can relax you a lot, and it releases the massive amount of tension you have in your body. Your laughter will also transfer to the audience. If you make the audience laugh at the beginning of your talk, they will be relaxed and more receptive to your ideas.

- **Remember, the beginning is the hardest.** If you get up on that stage, and you are shaking and nervous, remind yourself, "I just have to get past the two-minute mark."
After that, you will start to flow. It's always the first two minutes that are the hardest.

237

- **Finally, do not go into the restroom after you have a microphone on, but always use the bathroom beforehand.** You don't want a full-bladder on stage, but you also don't want the microphone on until after you have gone. You can imagine why.

Etiquette

There are a few "rules" of etiquette for speakers. Following them ensures you don't come across as rude, and that you get across your message in a memorable way. Always make your audience smarter and better for having known you. The wrong etiquette hinders this goal.

- **Never sell from stage.** If you're a thought leader, you're educating the audience with ideas, not selling a product or service. If you're giving a talk as a representative of a company, you're still not supposed to sell from stage. This upsets conference organizers and audiences alike. You can mention what your company is doing as a side note during a relevant part of the presentation, but any more than that will portray you as a used-car salesman.

- **Share the stage.** When you go to speak at an event where you are a panelist, meaning you are one of several speakers on stage, show respect by not being a time-hog. Keep your introduction between thirty seconds and a minute so as to not take away from others' intros. At a recent conference, there was a panelist who spoke for five minutes without taking a breath, rambling on about his company. Not only was it rude to the moderator, but it was boring and self-interested from the other panelists' and audiences' points of view.

- **Try to answer the given question.** I have been on panels where the moderator will ask a panelist a question and the panelist will practically ignore the question, spinning it around to talk about something else. The proper etiquette is to try and give a short, sweet answer to the moderator's actual question. When you ignore the moderator and are self-indulgent, you will likely not be asked back to the conference to speak ever again.

- **Never go over your time.** NEV-VER. Never. A friend of mine who is a speaker and speaker coach mentioned to me she "dies a little when she watches a speaker go over time." That's how I feel too. Conferences are on a tight schedule. Speakers are typically scheduled back to back, with little to no transition times between speakers. You should be so practiced that you never go over. If you do, you will be stealing time away from another speaker, from a break, or from something else previously scheduled. You might even make the event end late, which throws off the entire audience's schedules. If an event runs late, it could also cost the organizers more money for overtime space and employee charges. Be respectful by having your presentation practiced 100 percent before you step onto a stage.

Here are two tricks I use to never go over time. First, I plan the keynote to be one to two minutes shorter than the event indicates. For instance, if they tell me I should present a twenty-minute keynote, I plan and practice a nineteen-minute talk. No one will ever be upset that you came in one minute under; they will be relieved and happy you didn't go over. The second trick is to have your last slide be very flexible on how much time that content can take to explain. I always design my final slide to be explained in less than sixty seconds, but I can also spend two minutes, four minutes, even up to ten minutes explaining that one slide. With that type of extreme flexibility on your last slide, you should be able to come in exactly on time, every time.

- When you don't follow proper stage etiquette, which is all about being polite, then you will lose your audience. Furthermore, your chances to attend the conference in the future greatly decrease. I love to recommend other speakers, but when someone is self-indulgent and rude, I never recommend them. It is the fastest way to turn a major opportunity into a massive strike against yourself.

If you are ever asked to be a moderator for a panel, here are some great tips and tricks to have an interesting, relevant, and successful panel. Get relevant questions from the panelists before the conference or event. You can do this through a group call or email, though a call is much more effective. Make sure to ask the panelists what their individual goals are for the conference and intermingle those with what the conference's goals are. One trick is to ask panelists to write down three questions they can answer on stage, because this gives them room to showcase their expertise, and keeps the panel on topic and from going off on a tangent. You can always revise the questions they provide to fit better with the conference, but if you do, let the panelists know. Preparation is always the key to success.

Basic Needs

While every event should have everything you need, that's not always the case. Like everything else in life, there is a spectrum with some events being incredibly disorganized, or low budget, while some are five-star experiences. I typically bring a rolling computer bag with me, packed with the following essentials, just in case.

- A remote slide advancer (and check the batteries or charge it before you go).

- Your own laptop computer, even if they have one from which they are running all the presentations. Things happen; it's good to have the backup.

- A computer dongle to hook up your specific computer up to the projector. Different laptops use different connectors; it's not standardized. If you have to use your computer, even experienced AV teams may or may not have the right connectors, especially if you use a Mac.

- A backup USB drive with your presentation on it to give to the AV technicians.

- A bottle of water. There are many reasons you can get a dry mouth before you go on stage, from thirst and dehydration, to jet lag, medications, and plain old nerves. This will impact your ability to speak clearly. You don't want to have a severely dry mouth and have no water.

- Dry mouth spray, mouthwash, or gum to relieve dry mouth right before you go on stage (in addition to the water).

- Lip balm or gloss for dry lips, which can dramatically affect your speech.

- A protein snack because you cannot rely on being able to get food when you're at a conference. If things are delayed or running late, you could be starving, and your presentation will suffer for it. Bring a small snack, such as a banana, protein drink, or nuts. Make it something light that also keeps your blood sugar steady.

- Layers of clothes. Some stages are super hot, and some are super cold. Have options so you're not sweating or shivering on stage.

- Bring flats or comfortable shoes to slip into offstage. I learned this the hard way, after walking over six miles in one day in three-inch heels. It took me a week to recover! Some of these conferences are in buildings that are so gigantic, you end up walking for fifteen or twenty minutes once inside the building just to get to the stage. Places like Las Vegas, convention centers, and events with multiple stages or more than 1,000 people are the ones where you most likely have to walk great distances. Be prepared.

- Headache or allergy medicine.

Workbook Action Steps

We've covered a lot of ground when it comes to getting on stage. Here are few points to help you get started.

1. Set a goal. Either set a number of how many speaking engagements you want in the next one, two or three years (keynote, panel, or

moderator), or set a goal for your first speaking engagement by X date. Make it realistic, but still a stretch goal, and even put it on your calendar to reinforce your commitment.

2. Go back to the spreadsheet where you identified relevant events. Add in any additional events that might be a good fit, and choose ten that could be a good choice for your first speaking engagements

3. Apply to those identified events, either on the website, or use the organizing team's contact info on the website to email the team. This is a great task to outsource to your team or virtual assistants.

4. If you don't yet have a video of yourself giving a keynote, or at least on a panel, choose a way to get one recorded. If you have a video, skip this step.

   a. How will you get that first video? Choose now whether to film a video in your office or home, or if you need to rent a space for a few hours.

   b. Decide whether you are going to have anyone in the audience (friends) and reach out to them. If you plan on filming without an audience, you might want to add an audience track in editing.

   c. Set the date on your calendar to record the video.

   d. Choose a video editor or, if you are planning on doing it yourself, get video editing software. I typically use virtual assistants for this type of task.

5. Optional: Hire someone to help you get on stage. Pay a flat fee or percentage of the closed speaking engagements. Here's the hack: find a speaker who has been on appropriate stages, or an event organizer with a relevant event network, and ask if you can hire them for introductions. Remember to make it worth their while; they likely haven't been hired for this before.

Chapter 10

· · · · · · · ● ● ● ● · · · · · · · ·

Time Management

I f you are fantastic at time management and have lots of available time in your day, feel free to skip this chapter. For the 90 percent of you that don't have tons of free time, read on for tips.

The one complaint that I hear over is that people have "no time" or have too many things in their lives to do already. How in the world do you fit creating and building a thought leader platform into your already overpacked life?

By applying time management skills, hacks, and systems to your entire life.

The foundational secret of my success is that I treat my life as a business. I told you this in the beginning; I don't differentiate between having a personal and professional life. Every aspect of my life works together to achieve my life goals. I just have one life that includes my entire world, *Robin, Inc.* One of the most important ways to make sure you are approaching your own life as *You, Inc.*, with everything as one, is to manage how you spend your time on a day-to-day basis.

Outsourcing

Yes, I want to emphasize outsourcing one more time. It's that important.

Think about your time as currency. In economics, this is called opportunity cost, which can be measured in money, time, resources of any kind, or even by missed opportunity. In very basic language, everything you do, every dime you spend, every choice you make directs and commits certain resources, so those same resources can't be used in other ways.

How much time did you spend designing your last presentation slides? Five hours? Ten hours? How about grocery shopping this past month, or editing your last article? If these tasks take you a lot of time and you don't love doing them, you need to find ways to spend your time more wisely. Today, it's easy and inexpensive to delegate tasks and responsibilities.

> **Choose the top five things you're best at and outsource the rest.**

Sometimes, I get pushback about outsourcing everyday tasks. Some people say they like shopping for their groceries. I think, really? You like that more than you like an extra forty-five minutes of sleep, or an hour with your children? What do you have to sacrifice in order to physically go to the grocery store? If you're worried about quality, simply order from a high-end store.

Others who hire freelancers might worry that their tasks won't be done the same way they would do them. The truth is that freelancers don't always do great work. Sometimes, you'll need to sift through a few to find the right one. That said, you always have to consider the big picture and focus on maximizing your return on investment. Does the task need to be done exactly as you would do it? Could you let go of some of the smaller responsibilities, as long as you can keep moving forward doing what's truly important to you? Micromanaging and perfection are the enemies of time efficiency.

As I've mentioned throughout this book, I use Upwork and TaskRabbit to get many of my tasks accomplished, from cleaning closets to designing new PowerPoint decks, and more. On these platforms, you simply post a job, get a handful of applicants, and hire and manage via the platform. My other favorite on-demand resource is a subscription service for virtual assistants called Leverage. For a monthly subscription, I have a team of VAs on demand. I've had them do everything from editing videos, to formatting a database, to making travel arrangements, to reading an article before submitting it to *Forbes*.

Outsourcing should feel freeing. You no longer have to waste time on tasks that someone else can do better, faster, or well enough. Stay in line with your goals, have an overall project plan, and then choose what to keep and what to outsource.

Eisenhower's Matrix

To manage your time effectively, start with the basics, using President Eisenhower's "Time Management Matrix." The matrix is made up of four quadrants and helps you stay organized. Using the matrix, you can divide things in your life into the following categories:

- Urgent/important

- Not urgent/important

- Urgent/not important

- Not urgent/not important

	Urgent	Not Urgent
Important	Do Now	Schedule for Later
Not Important	Outsource	Delete

In quadrant one is the urgent and most important elements of your life. That's what you do first. Quadrant two is not urgent, but important. Here, you focus on your long-term goals. Quadrant three is not important, but urgent. The goal is to minimize this list as much as possible because it's a distraction. You can delegate a lot of this. Then quadrant four is not important and not urgent. Ignore things in this list, because they're time wasters with no ROI. Eliminate them.

If you fill out the four quadrants and you still feel like you have a ton in urgent and important, then prioritize them by ROI. Go after the biggest moneymakers first. Also remember that just because something is in your urgent and important quadrant doesn't mean you can't outsource it. Outsource as much as possible that you don't love doing.

Where Are You Spending Your Time?

Next, learn to master your calendar. Your calendar should reflect your goals. It's not about the amount of work you get done; it's the impact you make. Sometimes, you will need to say no to things, and that's okay. Stay focused on your overarching goal. Warren Buffet once said, "The difference between successful people and very successful people, is that very successful people say 'no' to almost everything."

> ## Very successful people say NO to almost everything.

If you're always too busy and you don't know where to cut things out, I encourage you to use the one-week calendar challenge. Put everything you do daily in your digital calendar or keep it in a list online. When I say everything, I mean everything. At the end of the week, you want to be able to see where you are spending your time.

Include exercise, errands, showers, getting dressed, meals, transportation, time on email, time on social media, phone calls, meetings, shopping, relaxing, sleeping, interacting, and even taking care of the animals. There's no judgment in this. Only you will see this. What is important is that this is your life, and you should be empowered to design it the way you want to design it. This just puts you in total control of *You, Inc.* If you want to spend three hours a day relaxing, then design your life so you have that.

At the end of the week, look and see where you're wasting time, what can be outsourced, or what can be cut out. Is your commute taking too much time? You can choose to take action. You could rearrange your drive time to be during non-rush hour, carpool, use the trains and buses, or telecommute. Some things might jump out as super obvious. If you spend three hours a week in total cleaning, then it's worth it to hire someone to take that over. You might need to spend money, but that is to be expected.

Your goal is to build your career or business, outsourcing what you might have thought of as personal tasks but are now assigned business metrics. Everything can be thought of as a business expense, and an investment in *You, Inc.* This exercise helps you achieve whatever goals you have by finding the hours you need in a day. The goal is to work less and achieve more impact.

Time Is Currency

Remember that time is currency. Get creative. If time is currency, it may make sense to invest in a home gym because doing so saves you hours each month in commute time, cost, and effort if you use a fitness center. If parking, driving, and DMV hassles are wasting hours a week, maybe selling your car and only using rideshare services may make sense. As I shared earlier, I decided to do exactly that and sold my car almost three years ago.

If time is currency, it makes sense to focus on doing the top five things you love doing that tie to your goals. In this way, you can, as Brendon Burchard says, "design your life."

As you're considering where you're spending your time, form a "no-brainer checklist." On this checklist, mark areas of your time you can automate: auto billing, auto deposit, online grocery shopping, or systematizing your mornings. Look at repetitive things you do and see if they can be simplified. For instance, instead of opening a bottle each day for your medication, get a weekly pill dispenser. Fill it every Sunday when you take your pill. When you make time saving a habit, you'll see the time saved add up to noticeable amounts.

What are the tasks stopping you from succeeding? Most of us are not procrastinators when it comes to things we love doing. If I am procrastinating, I know right away it's because I'm doing something I don't love to do. So, I find a way to outsource it. This is part of my "hack everything" mindset. It's a way of thinking that helps you find the easiest and most streamlined solutions to accomplish your goals.

Hacks

There are few specific hacks I have found useful for managing my time.

Time-Hacking Tip #1: Block-off time is foundational. I block off three hours in the morning every day. If possible, I don't schedule any meetings before 10:30 a.m. This routine is important to my life because of my chronic health issues. I wake up and spend forty-five minutes replying to email and reading news, with a small breakfast. I spend the next one hour, twenty minutes in my home gym; there is no wait, no commute, no distractions. If traveling, I make sure the hotel has a gym on site. Then I spend about fifty minutes showering, getting things together for the day, and eating another small breakfast. I do this seven days a week, whether I'm traveling or home. This sets up my every single day for success. You might need your own block-off times for your own reasons.

Time-Hacking Tip #2: Copy and paste is your friend. It saves you considerably more time than you think. Keep the spreadsheet up to date with template language for bios, descriptions, and more. Then remember to use it. I keep a Word doc open with general copy/paste language I use frequently. The huge bonus is that repetition makes your brand and message memorable, as we discussed in Chapter 6.

Time-Hacking Tip #3: Use the 90 percent rule. I live by this rule, a rule from the world of entrepreneurship. If it's 90 percent done, then it's done. If you try to achieve that extra 10 percent to make something perfect, you will fail, or the last 10 percent will require a significant amount of time and resources. When my first book was finished, I read over it twice, not ten times, not even three times. I moved on to my next order of business, because building a thought leader platform is the same as building a business. Silicon Valley VC Reid Hoffman famously said about startups: "If you're not embarrassed by the first version of your product, you've launched too late." We cannot afford perfection.

Perfection equals failure and is your enemy. Large corporations might strive for something closer to perfection, because they have the resources to do so. Startups don't have that luxury, and as a new thought leader, you're building a startup. Get your work to the 90 percent level, and then move on. As you do, you will realize just how true the Pareto principle is; 80 percent of the results do come from 20 percent of the input.

Time-Hacking Tip #4: Make decisions and seize opportunities. Delayed decisions lead to inaction, which leads to lost opportunity.

People often face three major obstacles in this area:

- Fast decision-making skills you can rely on

- The courage to take the leap

- The time it takes to grab that opportunity

Sometimes, what is causing the anxiety about making a decision are the potential ramifications much further in the future, at least ten or more decisions out. Your brain can go down crazy paths when imaging consequences or results. To counteract this anxiety, take one step at a time. Do not worry about one year from now. Delayed decisions lead to inaction, which leads to lost opportunity.

Reducing the amount of information bouncing around in your head allows you to focus on the ramifications of one decision. Again, the key is to take one step at a time.

When you're trying to make a decision, filling out this checklist—also found at the end of the chapter in the Action Items section—can help direct you to the right answer.

1. Consequences of the decision

2. Consequences of not making the decision

3. Factors that have a direct impact on the decision

4. Goals and what could happen by making the decision

Time-Hacking Tip #5: Use "Robin's five-minute rule" to create habits. When you want to create something new, like an exercise habit, you must commit to doing it five minutes a day for one week. Then gradually add minutes. Go to ten minutes a day, then fifteen minutes a day. By starting small, then gradually increasing, the task is easier to accomplish. Because the first two minutes of doing anything are the hardest, you may find you greatly surpass five minutes that first week.

Time-Hacking Tip #6: I like to live by the rule of "finish the small task." If a task takes less than two minutes to complete, do it now. For example, instead of putting your dirty dish in the sink, rinse it and put it in the dishwasher. Instead of letting your inbox pile up, jot off a quick response to as many emails as you can in that two-minute time frame. By taking immediate action, it doesn't pile up on your to-do list, and you actually save time in the long run.

Time-Hacking Tip #7: Simplify your environment. Clutter is a major enemy of efficient time management. It's easier to lose things in a cluttered environment, and you spend considerable time moving your stuff around and taking care of it. Ask yourself: do you manage your possessions, or do your possessions manage you?

Right now, grab two large boxes or bags, walk round your house, and grab anything you don't want anymore. Simply get rid of it by donating it, giving it away, or throwing it away. If you can't get rid of it because of sentimental value, then put it in a box to store it. Everyone has at least two full garbage bags of stuff they really should eliminate—knickknacks, magazines, books you'll never read again, clothes that don't fit or are stained, anything that has been sitting aside waiting for you to clean or fix for a long time. Your goal here is purely to eliminate, not organize or fix. The fewer possessions you have, the easier your life is to manage.

Workbook Action Steps

Now it's time to put what you've learned about time management into action.

1. Pick one tip in this chapter and start practicing. This entire chapter all relates back to the concept of clearing your space, whether that's your physical space or your mental space. Every small task and responsibility can add stress and pressure to your life. As the list

gets longer, you become more overwhelmed. At some point, you must ask yourself, "Do I manage my time, or does it manage me?"

2. Use the decision worksheet whenever you have to make a decision. Take only five minutes to complete this worksheet, use an actual timer. This will prevent you from thinking too much or going down what I call the "rabbit hole of what-ifs." The worksheet questions help you see the consequences of the decision versus the consequences of not making a decision. In the end, you can discover where your anxieties lie, and you can counteract them with structured information. Take it one step at a time.

   a. What's the decision to be made?

   b. What other things do you need to consider?

   c. If you decide to do this, what would be the immediate consequences?

   d. What would the consequences be if you delayed the decision?

   e. What's the best thing that could come from your decision?

f. After answering questions one through five, what fears or anxieties do you still have around your decision?

g. Write your decision here:

_____

Conclusion:
You're on Your Way!

The road to becoming a thought leader requires planning, commitment, strategy, and hard work. If you work hard, and build yourself like a business, with the capital and talent that is required, you will succeed.

Remember, it took me a few years of deep, hard, focused work, and learning hacks to get where I am today.

In this line of work, you will hear no often. You will need the support of others, and sometimes others will say no. You can't take it personally. In my work as a business development and sales professional, I'm turned down or told no more times in an average month than most people are in their entire lives. What I've found is that in business, no just means your business goals are not aligned at that point in time.

Expect to be turned down more than you're told yes. If you're not, maybe you aren't reaching high enough. Every time you hear no, remind yourself that this is completely normal.

As well as being told no, I can't stress enough how important it is to learn how to say no. When you say yes to some things, you have to sacrifice others. That is the opportunity cost of time. Think about what you are giving up and weigh your options. Use Eisenhower's Matrix to make clear, concise decisions without fear or anxiety. Take a look at what you dropped from your calendar already, and remind yourself if you say yes, you have to say no to other things that probably should be a greater priority. Don't let other people decide your schedule or what you do with your time by saying yes to all the requests you hear. This includes some potential speaking engagements that might not be worth your time.

Definitely say yes if the opportunity outweighs the consequences. I prefer to jump into the deep end of the ocean, instead of slowly descending into the shallow end of the pool. There will always be a risk of failure, and if you never fully immerse yourself into the things you need to do to accomplish your goal, you will never make it as a thought leader.

Closing Notes on Bullying and Bias

Everywhere you turn, there will always be a bully (or several). When you make it big, that won't change. In fact, some people may become considerably more vicious. The best thing you can do for yourself is walk away. My trick is to never look back at my abusers; I cut all negative people and influences out of my life completely.

Don't fight against the negativity; let it go. Play your game, not theirs. If you're being pushed down or don't feel there is room for advancement where you are, bide your time and wait until you have a foundation in place to leave. If you've hit a glass ceiling and people see you only at that level, it's time to move on.

New Opportunities Await

With your new platform, new doors will open for you. Soon enough, a new opportunity will fall into your lap each day. Just remember that this is a marathon, not a sprint. Make a plan. Put action items on your calendar. And move ahead one step at a time. You'll get out what you put in.

Thought leadership will accentuate and accelerate whatever you're doing in your life. If you don't love what you're doing now, then becoming a thought leader is the right move to make. It gives you both safety and opportunity now and in our future world of work.

If you didn't fill out the worksheets I provided along the way, go back and do them now. These will help you define and build your *You, Inc.* foundation and launch into your first vertical. There is no pressure to be perfect. This is your first draft of your thought leader foundation, and it will change. That's fine. All success begins with taking those first, hard steps.

Remember, I'm rooting for you! Good luck with your exciting journey and go ahead and tag me with your progress on social media!

About the Author

Robin Farmanfarmaian is a professional speaker, having now completed over one hundred speaking engagements in twelve countries. She is also an entrepreneur and angel investor, driving high-level business development for cutting-edge medical and biotech companies poised to impact one hundred million people or more. Currently, Farmanfarmaian is VP of Actavalon, curing cancer; strategic relations advisor to MindMaze, VR for stroke and brain injury rehabilitation; and on the board of directors for New Scholars, focusing on the intersection of AI and education. Her recent investments include Invicta Medical, a medical technology company for sleep apnea, and Dance Biopharm, inhaled insulin with a smart, connected device.

Robin is on the board of directors or advisory board of many startups and conferences and works with entrepreneurs and executives who want to become thought leaders. A lifelong philanthropist and mentor, she was the cofounder and on the board of directors (formally executive director) for the Organ Preservation Alliance, catalyzing breakthroughs in organ banking for transplants and tissue engineering. Other previous work includes being one of the founders of Morfit, the Exponential Medicine conference, President at Innovation for Jobs, a nonprofit cofounded by Vint Cerf, and a VP at Singularity University. Her book, *The Patient as CEO: How Technology Empowers the Healthcare Consumer,* is a #1 Best Seller on Amazon.